# MILITARY FAMILIES

## Families Today

Adoptive Families

Disability and Families

Foster Families

Homelessness and Families

Immigrant Families

Incarceration and Families

LGBT Families

Military Families

Multigenerational Families

Multiracial Families

Single-Parent Families

Teen Parents

Families Today

# MILITARY FAMILIES

H.W. Poole

MASON CREST

Mason Crest
450 Parkway Drive, Suite D
Broomall, PA 19008
www.masoncrest.com



MTM Publishing, Inc.
435 West 23rd Street, #8C
New York, NY 10011
www.mtmpublishing.com

President: Valerie Tomaselli
Vice President, Book Development: Hilary Poole
Designer: Annemarie Redmond
Copyeditor: Peter Jaskowiak
Editorial Assistant: Andrea St. Aubin

Series ISBN: 978-1-4222-3612-3
Hardback ISBN: 978-1-4222-3620-8
E-Book ISBN: 978-1-4222-8264-9

Library of Congress Cataloging-in-Publication Data
Names: Poole, Hilary W., author.
Title: Military families / by H.W. Poole.
Description: Broomall, PA : Mason Crest [2017] | Series: Families Today | Includes index.
Identifiers: LCCN 2016008342| ISBN 9781422236208 (hardback) | ISBN 9781422236123 (series) | ISBN 9781422282649 (e-book)
Subjects: LCSH: Families of military personnel—United States—Juvenile literature. | Children of military personnel—United States—Juvenile literature. | United States—Armed Forces—Military life—Juvenile literature.
Classification: LCC UB403 .P66 2017 | DDC 355.1/20973—dc23
LC record available at http://lccn.loc.gov/2016008342

Printed and bound in the United States of America.

First printing
9 8 7 6 5 4 3 2 1

# TABLE OF CONTENTS



## Key Icons to Look for:

**Words to Understand:** These words with their easy-to-understand definitions will increase the reader's understanding of the text, while building vocabulary skills.

**Sidebars:** This boxed material within the main text allows readers to build knowledge, gain insights, explore possibilities, and broaden their perspectives by weaving together additional information to provide realistic and holistic perspectives.

**Research Projects:** Readers are pointed toward areas of further inquiry connected to each chapter. Suggestions are provided for projects that encourage deeper research and analysis.

**Text-Dependent Questions:** These questions send the reader back to the text for more careful attention to the evidence presented there.

**Series Glossary of Key Terms:** This back-of-the-book glossary contains terminology used throughout the series. Words found here increase the reader's ability to read and comprehend higher-level books and articles in this field.

In the 21st century, families are more diverse than ever before.

# SERIES INTRODUCTION

Our vision of "the traditional family" is not nearly as time-honored as one might think. The standard of a mom, a dad, and a couple of kids in a nice house with a white-picket fence is a relic of the 1950s—the heart of the baby boom era. The tumult of the Great Depression followed by a global war caused many Americans to long for safety and predictability—whether such stability was real or not. A newborn mass media was more than happy to serve up this image, in the form of TV shows like *Leave It To Beaver* and *The Adventures of Ozzie and Harriet*. Interestingly, even back in the "glory days" of the traditional family, things were never as simple as they seemed. For example, a number of the classic "traditional" family shows—such as *The Andy Griffith Show, My Three Sons,* and a bit later, *The Courtship of Eddie's Father*—were actually focused on single-parent families.

Sure enough, by the 1960s our image of the "perfect family" was already beginning to fray at the seams. The women's movement, the gay rights movement, and—perhaps more than any single factor—the advent of "no fault" divorce meant that the illusion of the Cleaver family would become harder and harder to maintain. By the early 21st century, only about 7 percent of all family households were traditional—defined as a married couple with children where *only* the father works outside the home.

As the number of these traditional families has declined, "nontraditional" arrangements have increased. There are more single parents, more gay and lesbian parents, and more grandparents raising grandchildren than ever before. Multiracial families—created either through interracial relationships or adoption—are also increasing. Meanwhile, the transition to an all-volunteer military force has meant that there are more kids growing up in military families than there were in the past. Each of these topics is treated in a separate volume in this set.

While some commentators bemoan the decline of the traditional family, others argue that, overall, the recognition of new family arrangements has brought more good than bad. After all, if very few people live like the Cleavers anyway, isn't it better to be honest about that fact? Surely, holding up the traditional family as an ideal to which all should aspire only serves to stigmatize kids whose lives differ from that standard. After all, no children can be held responsible for whatever family they find themselves in; all they can do is grow up as best they can. These books take the position that every family—no matter what it looks like—has the potential to be a successful family.

That being said, challenges and difficulties arise in every family, and nontraditional ones are no exception. For example, single parents tend to be less well off financially than married parents are, and this has long-term impacts on their children. Meanwhile, teenagers who become parents tend to let their educations suffer, which damages their income potential and career possibilities, as well as risking the future educational attainment of their babies. There are some 400,000 children in the foster care system at any given time. We know that the uncertainty of foster care creates real challenges when it comes to both education and emotional health.

Furthermore, some types of "nontraditional" families are ones we wish did not have to exist at all. For example, an estimated 1.6 million children experience homelessness at some point in their lives. At least 40 percent of homeless kids are lesbian, gay, bisexual, or transgender teens who were turned out of their homes because of their orientation. Meanwhile, the United States incarcerates more people than any other nation in the world—about 2.7 million kids (1 in 28) have an incarcerated parent. It would be absurd to pretend that such situations are not extremely stressful and, often, detrimental to kids who have to survive them.

The goal of this set, then, is twofold. First, we've tried to describe the history and shape of various nontraditional families in such a way that kids who aren't familiar with them will be able to not only understand, but empathize. We also present demographic information that may be useful for students who are dipping their toes into introductory sociology concepts.

Second, we have tried to speak specifically to the young people who are living in these nontraditional families. The series strives to address these kids as

**Meeting challenges and overcoming them together can make families stronger.**

sympathetically and supportively as possible. The volumes look at some of the typical problems that kids in these situations face, and where appropriate, they offer advice and tips for how these kids might get along better in whatever situation confronts them.

Obviously, no single book—whether on disability, the military, divorce, or some other topic—can hope to answer every question or address every problem. To that end, a "Further Reading" section at the back of each book attempts to offer some places to look next. We have also listed appropriate crisis hotlines, for anyone with a need more immediate than can be addressed by a library.

Whether your students have a project to complete or a problem to solve, we hope they will be able to find clear, empathic information about nontraditional families in these pages.

—H. W. Poole

Jessica Alba's father served in the Air Force and her grandfather was a Marine.

# Chapter One

# SOLDIERS AND FAMILIES

The following celebrities have something in common—do you know what it is? Actors Jessica Alba and Mark Hamill, sports stars Mia Hamm and Tiger Woods, *Hunger Games* author Suzanne Collins, and musicians Ciara, Trey Songz, and Christina Aguilera.

Answer? They are all military brats.

The term might sound like an insult, but it isn't meant that way. Within the military, "brat" is actually an affectionate way of talking about kids in military families. The lives of kids who have a parent (or parents) in the military are often

## Words to Understand

**civilian:** not military.

**dependents:** people (usually family members) who rely on someone for financial and other support.

**enlisted:** people who have signed up for military service.

**personnel:** workers, staff members, or in the military, soldiers.

**reserve:** in the military, people who are trained and ready to support the military when needed.

different from "average" kids in some important ways. So the term *military brat* is a kind of badge of honor for kids who have grown up in that environment.

But before we get to that, let's look at how the U.S. military is organized and who military families are.

## OVERVIEW OF THE MILITARY

The U.S. military has five branches: Army, Navy, Air Force, Marines, and Coast Guard. Each branch has its own responsibilities. People usually associate the Army with what's called "ground troops," while the Air Force is associated with planes, and the Navy and Coast Guard with ships. But the reality is somewhat more complicated than that, and there is plenty of overlap.

For example, although the Army and Air Force are different branches, the Army has its own pilots and uses helicopters in attacks. The Navy has pilots, too. There is also overlap between the activities of the Marines and the Navy. Meanwhile, the Marines *also* have their own planes and pilots. As its name suggests, the Coast Guard is primarily focused on protecting American waters, but during wartime, the Coast Guard can also be sent all over the world.

There are lively rivalries among the branches. (Just ask someone in the Navy who is better: Navy pilots or Air Force pilots!) But in practice all the branches work together to defend the United States at home and abroad.

All branches of the U.S. military have an active duty side and a **reserve** side. *Active duty* refers to people who are part of the military full time, while *reservists* are people who are trained and can be "called up" to service if needed. There is also a distinction between ***enlisted personnel*** and *officers*. Enlisted personnel make up about 82 percent of the military, and they carry out the operations. The remaining 18 percent are officers. Officers do the planning and management of military activities. They also perform certain specialized jobs, such as medicine.

When we think of "the military," we usually think of soldiers as they're shown in movies. But it's important to understand that the U.S. military is a huge

One example of the long rivalry between military branches is the famous Army–Navy football game, which has been played annually since 1890. Here the U.S. Naval Academy Midshipmen take the field in 2012.

organization. There are many service members who are not literally soldiers. They might be engineers, machine and vehicle operators, electricians, construction workers, and so on. The military also has its own health-care staff, which includes not only doctors, but also dentists, nurses, pharmacists, and physical therapists. The U.S. military has its own police force and even its own firefighters.

## THE MILITARY COMMUNITY

There are more than 3.6 million men and women in the U.S. military. That includes about 1.4 million active duty personnel and 1.1 million reservists, plus retired and

A Coast Guard officer looks for survivors after Hurricane Katrina. Both the National Guard and the Coast Guard were lauded for their efforts after the 2005 hurricane hit the Gulf Coast.

standby reservists, and **civilian** personnel. Broken down by branch, the numbers look like this:

- Army: about 530,000 on active duty.
- Air Force: about 325,000 on active duty.
- Navy: about 320,000 on active duty.
- Marine Corps: about 195,000 on active duty.
- Coast Guard: about 40,000 on active duty.

There is roughly one officer for every five enlisted personnel, although that varies slightly by branch.

There are more than 200,000 women on active duty, or just shy of 15 percent of the total force. In the reserve force, the percentage is slightly higher:

## The National Guard

In the earliest years of the United States, each state had its own militia to protect it. These state militias evolved into what's now known as the National Guard, which was formally organized in 1916. Both the Army and the Air Force have National Guards, which are commanded by the governors of their states. These troops are often brought in to help during crises. For example, more than 50,000 National Guard troops from various states were called in to help immediately after Hurricane Katrina, which killed more than 1,800 people along the Gulf Coast in 2005.

Although the National Guard is organized by state, members can also be "called up" by the federal government. In fact, the National Guard has a long history of service in America's foreign conflicts. For example, the majority of the soldiers in the Spanish American War were from the National Guard. The Guard also provided about 40 percent of the American force in World War I, and the Guard has been involved in every conflict since then. Since the terrorist attacks of 2001, the National Guard has been on the front lines of homeland defense, as well as being deployed to Afghanistan and Iraq.

Members of the National Guard commonly train about one weekend per month. The idea is to allow members to live fairly "normal" civilian lives, while also ensuring that soldiers are physically and mentally ready to serve at short notice.

If you have a parent in the National Guard, you probably notice that he or she has to be away every once in a while to train. Chances are you won't experience as much disruption in your life as active-duty military families do—unless, of course, the moment comes when your parent is deployed to a crisis or war.

18.5 percent of the reserve force is female. Thirty percent of active duty members describe themselves as a minority (black, Asian, etc.), while 11.6 percent of active duty force describe themselves as Hispanic. Among reservists, 25 percent describe themselves as racial minorities and 10 percent as Hispanic.

Slightly more than half of the people on active duty (55. 2 percent) are married. More officers are married (69.7 percent) than enlisted personnel (52.2 percent). And slightly less than half of reservists (45.9 percent) are married. Overall, 36.1 percent of military members are married with children, and 6.6 percent are single with children. There are about 2.2 million military personnel (both active and reservists) who are members of military families, and they have just under 3 million family members (spouses, children, and adult **dependents**).

Children of military families tend to be young. Of the 1.9 million military kids, 37.4 percent are under the age of 6; 30.8 percent are between 6 and 11 years

A taekwondo class for military kids at the Youth and Teen Center of Marine Corps Air Station Miramar, in San Diego, California.

Military families can often shop at their own commissaries, such as this one at Kadena Air Base in Okinawa, Japan.

old; 24.7 percent are between 12 and 18, and 7.1 percent are between 19 and 22. (of those over 18 years old, only those who are college students are counted as dependents by the military.)

## Text-Dependent Questions

1. What are the five branches of the U.S. military?
2. How many "military brats" are there?
3. What is the role of the National Guard?

## Research Project

Choose one of the five branches of the U.S. military and find out more about it. When was it founded and for what purpose? What are some of its major accomplishments? Write a history and/or create a timeline of key events.

A classic recruitment poster from World War II, when the U.S. military expanded very rapidly.

# Chapter Two

# A CHANGING FORCE

You might be surprised to learn that the idea of a "military family" is actually pretty new. For most of American history, the military was kept fairly small except during times of war.

## THE DRAFT

When Japan bombed the U.S. military base at Pearl Harbor in 1941, America quickly "ramped up" the military in order to enter World War II. There was a vast and swift increase in the number of enlisted people, as well as officers, doctors, engineers, and so on. Many people volunteered, while others were *drafted*—the United States reserves the right to conscript, or force, young men to fight in the army if necessary.

### Words to Understand

**commissary:** a store that sells supplies on a military base.

**deferment:** a postponement of military service.

**deployment:** when military service people are sent to a war zone.

**subsidy:** money that's given in order to assist someone with a particular job or activity.

About 3 million men were drafted in 1942, 3.3 million more were drafted in 1943, and about 1.5 million in 1944. After the war ended in 1945, the vast majority of soldiers returned home and went back to their regular lives.

The draft for World War II was the largest in American history. But the basic pattern for "smaller" wars has been similar. In the past, the military would expand during a war, using the draft, and then shrink back when it was over. So while there have always been people—mostly officers—who spent their lives in the military as a career, overall this was not a very large group.

This pattern changed for a few reasons. A big factor was the war in Vietnam. Unlike World War II, which was viewed by the majority of Americans as just and necessary, many people objected to America's involvement in Vietnam. Some young men volunteered to fight because they viewed it as their duty to support their country, but many didn't want to go. The draft was done by a lottery system at that time. Each young man was assigned a number, based on his birthday. If your number was chosen in the lottery, you had to go. However, there were a lot of exceptions made; these were called **deferments**. College students could avoid being drafted, for example, as could men with young children. Significantly, wealthy people with political connections were also able to avoid the draft.

A lot of people were angry. Some people didn't like the Vietnam War itself. Others didn't like that some people could get out of service while others couldn't. Some people didn't like the very idea of a country forcing people to fight wars in the first place. Even U.S. military lost faith in the idea of a draft. It turned out that forcing someone to become a soldier does not always create the best soldiers. There were a lot of "discipline problems" in the Army that many officers blamed on the draft.

Meanwhile, changes in population meant that a lot more young men were eligible for the draft than the military could ever actually use. And so, in 1973, the U.S. military became an all-volunteer force (AVF). Young men do still have to register for a possible draft (now called Selective Service), just in case it becomes necessary in the future. But since 1973, everyone serving in the military has volunteered to be there.

At an antiwar rally in 1970, a young man burns his draft card in protest.

## FAMILIES AND THE AVF

The transition to an AVF made for a huge change in the makeup of U.S. military. The average soldier has a higher IQ than during the draft and is more likely to have finished high school. There has also been a huge increase in the number of people who choose the military as a career. This has created a greater sense of professionalism than existed before. After all, if someone is drafted only for a year or so, he will have a very different attitude toward the job than someone who is planning to make a life in the military.

The AVF also inspired a huge expansion in the number of military families. When the military is a long-term career rather than as a short-term obligation, it makes sense that more people will want to have a family while serving. Increasing numbers of women in the military have also led to larger numbers of military families.

On the whole, people in the military get married at a younger age than civilians. They tend to have children earlier than civilians, and they tend to have more

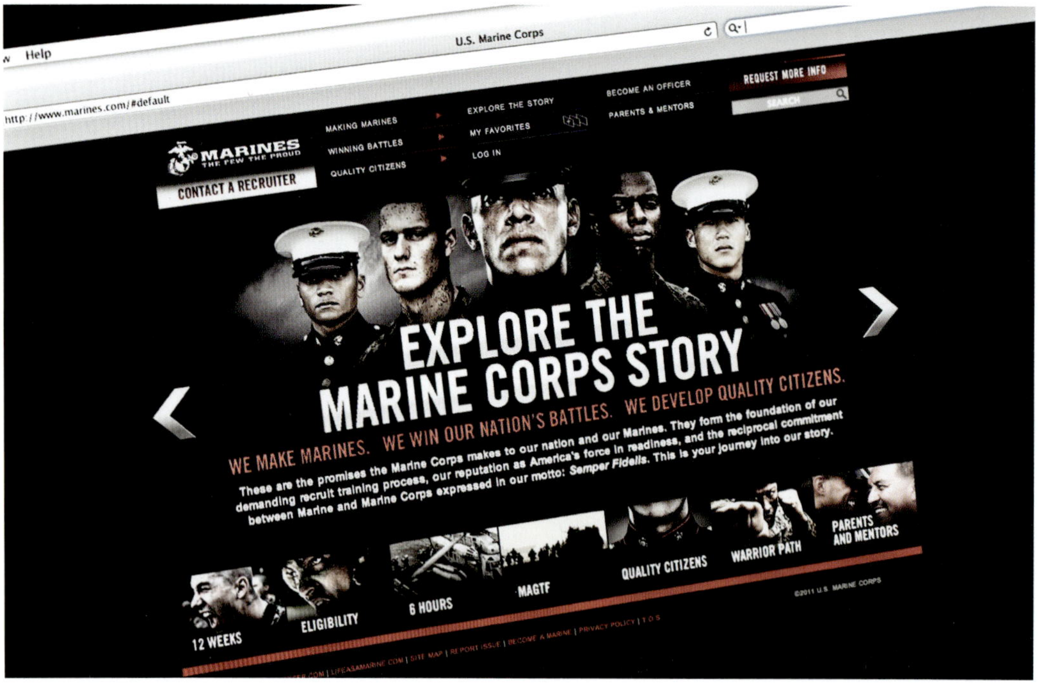


Since the transition to an AVF, the U.S. military has had to work hard to recruit new service people through advertising and other techniques.

children. In fact, family members now outnumber service people. In other words, there are more spouses and children associated with the military than there are people serving.

## MILITARY FAMILY LIFE

Because military service is now voluntary, people can leave if they want to. Research has shown that one of the most important factors in a service member's decision to stay in the military is how happy his or her spouse is. So the military has had to become more "family friendly" in order to keep more of its volunteer members.

For example, service members and their dependents can get health care, dental insurance, and life insurance. Family members can receive **subsidies** for continuing their educations or getting job training. On military bases, there are **commissaries** that sell discounted goods. Different branches of the military also have various programs to support military parents. For example, a program called Army Child and Youth Services provides affordable child care and after-school programs for Army kids. Another great perk for military families is called "space-available travel"—service members and their families can travel on military aircraft anywhere in the world, for free, as long as there are open seats. The military also offers discounted legal assistance and money-management advice to families who need it.

Still, there are many aspects of the military that can never be "family friendly." A big part of life for enlisted people is **deployment**, which is when a soldier or other service member is sent to a war zone. Deployment creates a lot of stress for military families, which will be discussed more in chapter three. Even when an enlisted person is not deployed, he or she is likely to move on a fairly regular basis. See chapter four for more on moving.

## Text-Dependent Questions

1. What was the draft?
2. When and why was the draft ended?
3. How has the U.S. military changed since the draft ended?

## Research Project

Choose two major American wars and compare and contrast how the military functioned during those conflicts. Where did the recruits come from: were they volunteers or conscripted? How were the soldiers treated when they came back: as heroes or villains?

The moment when they have to say goodbye can be really hard for military kids.

# Chapter Three

# DEPLOYMENT AND REUNION

Terrorists belonging to a group called al-Qaeda attacked the United States on September 11, 2001, killing almost 3,000 people. The United States has been at war ever since. There have been two main operations in the Middle East: Operation Enduring Freedom in Afghanistan and Operation Iraqi Freedom in Iraq. In addition to the campaigns in the Middle East, American troops have also been sent on various missions to Somalia, Cuba, and Haiti, among other places.

One effect of the switch to an all-volunteer forces is that more is expected of the people who do volunteer. Longer deployments, lasting six months or more, are common, and the number of multiple deployments has increased. Multiple deployments refers to being sent to a war ("a tour"), coming home for a while, and

## Words to Understand

**empathize:** to understand how someone else is feeling, even if you have never been in that exact situation.

**psychologist:** a doctor who specializes in mental or emotional issues.

**veteran:** a former member of the armed services.

then being sent back for an additional tour. This all has significant effects, not only on the soldiers themselves, but also on the family members who stay behind.

## GETTING READY

Some military families say that the time just before deployment is actually harder than the deployment itself. First, parents have a lot of practical things they need to do. They need to make budgets, figure out how child care will work, and make various other plans.

The idea of your mom or dad being deployed is pretty scary. Talk to your parent about what worries you.

But the real stress is emotional. If your parent is about to be deployed, you may spend a lot of time thinking and worrying about what will happen to him or her. You might also worry about what your daily life will be like when you only have one parent to look after you. And for kids of single parents, the worry can be even worse: Will you live with a grandparent? Other family members? What will that be like?

## Tips for Families

The website Military OneSource (www.militaryonesource.mil) has some tips on what military families can do to make the deployment easier. These include:

- Make plans and keep busy.
- Volunteer. It might sound strange, but one of the best ways to make yourself feel better is to help out somebody else.
- Spend time with other families in the same situation as you.
- Focus on what you can control. It's totally understandable that you are worried about your parents' safety. But you can't do anything about that. What can you control? Spending time with your family or friends? Helping out your mom and dad with things around the house? Engage in school activities or take up a new hobby?
- Find out more about stress management techniques and try some out. Some people find that exercise helps, while others like writing in journals. Not every technique works for everybody, and that's okay.
- Be honest about how you feel. You might be worried, upset, or stressed out. You might feel angry that your parent isn't around. That's all totally okay. You know what else is okay? Feeling happy. You aren't required to be depressed the entire time your parent is gone. Your parent wants you to get by as best you can. He or she *wants* you to feel happy, so try not to feel guilty if you do.

Make plans about how you'll keep in touch while your parent is away.

One thing you learn as you get older is that waiting for something to happen is often worse than actually going through it. Our minds have ways of making future situations seem worse that they turn out to be. For that reason, it helps to have an open family discussion about the deployment. Your parent may not be able to answer every single question you have—in fact, he or she might not be *allowed* to tell you everything! But you can get a lot of your questions answered. You can also talk about your fears or frustrations, discuss what life is going to be like during the deployment, and make a plan for keeping in touch while your parent is away (such as e-mail, letters, video chat, and so on).

The good news is that a lot of families have been through this before. Take advantage of their knowledge if you can. Most branches of the military offer "pre-deployment events" for families, where you can talk to people who have already had these experiences. Taking the mystery out of the situation can make a big difference.

## REUNION

As soon as a deployment begins, both soldiers and family members start thinking about when it will end—that great day when the family can be reunited again. And there's no question that reunions are a very happy time for military families. However, they can also be very stressful; oftentimes, they are more stressful than anyone ever expected.

Consider those first days and weeks after the family member has gotten home. The soldier has just left what was most likely an incredibly stressful

Experts suggest that families should talk openly about what the service member wants and needs when he or she gets home. Some veterans enjoy having a fuss made over them, but others do not.

situation. Families may want to celebrate by having lots of friends visit, or maybe by taking a trip somewhere special. But a returning soldier may need "downtime" to just be quiet and process what has happened. Throwing a big party, or being dragged to Disneyland, may be the opposite of what the **veteran** needs when he or she first gets home.

On the other hand, sometimes soldiers do want to celebrate when they come home. In fact, it may feel like they want to visit with everyone they've ever met! Meanwhile, kids have been missing their moms and dads, so they might just want some alone time with them.

## Dealing with Grief

It is terrible when kids lose a parent for any reason. Losing a parent to war can be especially heartbreaking. Partly this is because of the frequently violent nature of the death. Also, there is something more "public" about a military death. It may be mentioned on the news, for example, which means lots of people might want to talk to you about it. You might like that, or you might *really* not. Both reactions are totally normal.

For more information and help about grief, you might try these sources:

- **The Dougy Center:** http://www.dougy.org/grief-resources/help-for-kids.
- **KidsHealth:** http://kidshealth.org/parent/emotions/feelings/death.html.
- **Mental Health America:** http://www.mentalhealthamerica.net/conditions/bereavement-and-grief-information-military-families-and-communities.
- **Sesame Street for Military Families (for very young kids):** http://www.sesamestreetformilitaryfamilies.org.

There's no "correct" reaction here—not for parents coming home from deployment, and not for their spouses or kids who are welcoming them. All of these conflicting wishes can be worked out if everyone is patient and just listens to everyone else. But it can be hard when everybody wants different things.

Experts suggest that the initial homecoming should only include close family. Then, afterward, the returning soldier should be able to decide how quickly or slowly he or she wants to greet everyone else. The **psychologist** Dr. Terry Lyles says, "The biggest thing is not letting [the veteran] feel he has no control. . . . He's just left a deployment. The last thing he needs is to be deployed to a party. It's OK for him to come home and say, 'I'm not going to do anything.' That's healthy."

Dr. Lyles compares coming home from a war to a wife being pregnant. What he means is that, if a wife is pregnant, the husband needs to be patient and **empathize** with his wife—even though he has no way of knowing exactly what she is going through. According to Dr. Lyles, living with a veteran is quite similar. Family members need to empathize as best they can, while realizing that they'll never fully know what the war experience was like.

## BACK TO NORMAL

After the initial joy of reunion wears off, it's time to go back to "normal" life. Some families find this to be the toughest part. Everyone involved will have changed during the period of deployment, which means things probably won't be exactly the same as they were before.

It's most obvious how the soldier has changed—he or she has been at war. First of all, day-to-day life in a war zone is very different from civilian life. Expectations about behavior and even language are very different. When someone has gotten used to being in danger on a regular basis, it can feel very strange to be home. It's great that there is less danger, but it is also confusing at times, because it's not what you are used to. Soldiers need to, essentially, relearn how to be civilians, and that includes relearning how to be moms and dads.

A homecoming ceremony for troops with the 3rd Infantry Division's 4th Brigade Combat Team in 2008.

Sometimes other emotions are difficult to deal with, too. For example, those coming back from a long deployment may feel guilty about having missed so much time with their kids. They may also be coping with physical injuries or with the emotional effects of being in combat (see chapter four).

Meanwhile, the family at home will also have changed. Kids get older, for one thing. The five-year-old who waved goodbye to Daddy might be six or even older by the time he comes back. A year or so isn't much for adults, but kids can change a huge amount in that time. You may be a pretty different person from the one your parent remembers. You both will need to get to know each other again.

Meanwhile the parents who stayed home (usually moms, but not always), get used to handling daily life on their own. Suddenly, there is another adult around again, someone who has needs and desires and needs to be included. Although it's obviously a great thing to have him or her back, sharing household responsibilities again can be a big adjustment.

Experts say that the first thing to do about this situation is just to be aware of it. Talk openly about what's going on. Also, make sure you set aside some fun "family time," to enjoy an activity together. Eat dinner together. Get help with homework. And, most of all, be patient—everyone in the family needs time to get used to each other again.

## Text-Dependent Questions

1. What is involved in the pre-deployment period?
2. What are some tips for getting by while a family member is deployed?
3. What are some of the tensions that might come up after a service member comes home?

## Research Project

Find out more about the experience of deployment. Read advice from people who have been through it, and find out about services offered to military families in your area. You can start with the sources listed at the end of this book, and you can also look online for more. You might start with sites like Military OneSource (http://www.militaryonesource.mil). Create a booklet that could be shared with someone whose family member is deployed.

Fighting the enemy is far from the only thing service people do. These members of the 1151st Engineer Company are constructing a building as part of Forward Operation Base Lightning in Afghanistan.

# Chapter Four

# SPECIAL CHALLENGES

Only about 1 percent of the U.S. population is on active duty in the U.S. military. If you add in all the reservists and civilian employees, you still only get between 3 and 4 percent of the population. In other words, no more than 4 percent of Americans are charged with protecting and defending the other 96 percent. That's a big burden, and unfortunately the kids of that 4 percent carry some of that burden, too.

The previous chapter discussed some of the stress that deployment can put on a family. But there are other issues as well. One is the frequent moves,

## Words to Understand

**alienated:** a feeling of distance from others.

**amputation:** when a body part, such as an arm or a leg, is cut off.

**caregiving:** looking after someone who needs a lot of help.

**distress:** suffering.

which lead to a sense of separateness between military brats and civilian kids. And another, unfortunately, is the burden of **caregiving** that falls on military families in cases of injury or mental **distress**.

## CHANGE OF STATION

Frequently, service members will only be stationed at a particular military base for a set period of time, and then they will be sent to a different base. This is often called PCS, for *permanent change of station*. And if service members move, their families usually move with them. On average, military families move every two to three years; that's about 2.4 times more often than civilian families. Military families also move greater distances than civilians do.

These PCSs make sense to people who run the military, but they can be hard on families. Frequent moves can have a negative effect on child development, because moving interrupts school and can end friendships. Moving frequently also damages the other parent's ability to find work. On average, military spouses tend to be better educated than civilians, but they have higher rates of unemployment. When they do get jobs, they tend to earn less than civilians. A lot of this is directly related to the frequent moves.

Depending on where and how often they move, kids who grow up in the military sometimes feel **alienated** from civilian culture. That's especially true for kids who spend a lot of time on military bases in foreign countries. They don't really get to know the way civilian people live; instead, they really only know the life on the base.

On the positive side, a lot of military brats say that they grew up more independent and confident. They get used to being thrown into new situations, so they don't fear change. It can be hard to make new friends every few years—but the positive side is that military brats get pretty good at it! Also, the military itself is a tight-knit community. According to the website Military Brat Life, "we (all of us associated with the military) really are family!"

Kids participate in a sack race as part of Fourth of July celebrations at the Little Rock Air Force Base.

## POST-TRAUMATIC STRESS DISORDER

Although being in a military family is great in many ways, there are some hard parts that sometimes can't be avoided. The reality is that some people who go

A National Guardsman who served two tours in Iraq greets Roscoe, a companion dog that was trained to help the veteran with his PTSD.

to war don't come back. Fortunately, that happens a very small percentage of the time. But it does happen, and it's totally natural for family members to be frightened about it. It's important to remember that medical care on the battlefield has never been better than it is right now, and doctors are able to save many more soldiers than ever before.

Another terrible aspect of deployment is the effect that war often has on human beings. Military families are more likely than civilian families to be affected by a condition called post-traumatic stress disorder (PTSD). PTSD is caused by exposure—especially repeated exposure—to extremely frightening situations.

Although people sometimes talk about PTSD as though it is a new thing, emotional and mental trauma from war is actually as old as war itself. Herodotus, a Greek historian from ancient times, wrote about a general who chose to *not* send some of his troops back to war because they were too traumatized by what they had seen.

According to the U.S. Department of Veterans Affairs, somewhere between 11 to 20 percent of those who served in Iraq or Afghanistan have PTSD. Symptoms of PTSD include:

- difficulty sleeping
- difficulty concentrating
- feeling stressed out or tense for no obvious reason
- feeling guilty or depressed
- feeling "numb" with no emotion at all
- sharp changes in mood, such as being very quick to anger
- nightmares and scary thoughts
- flashbacks, where people relive the traumatic experiences over and over in their minds

PTSD is obviously very hard for the person experiencing it, but it can be almost as tough on their families. The condition can make sufferers seem like they are not even the same people they used to be—this is upsetting and confusing for kids and spouses. Family members might feel alienated from the veteran or even afraid of him or her. It's common to feel depressed and angry about the entire situation.

But it's important to understand that PTSD can be treated. Medication and therapy are both important and useful ways to address the disorder. Doctors and therapists are learning more about PTSD every year, and the treatment options are growing and becoming more effective.

## Learning from War

There's an old song that asks what war is good for, and then the lyrics answer "absolutely nothing." But the many wars America has fought have led to at least one positive outcome: major advances in medicine.

During the Vietnam War, the injury doctors treated most often was the gunshot wound. When American doctors came home from the war, the field of emergency medicine was almost completely overhauled. Today we all benefit from the techniques military doctors learned in Vietnam.

The wars in Afghanistan and Iraq also had their unique injuries. Soldiers had less concern about being shot, but much more concern about bombs. Most of these bombs were *improvised explosive devices*, or IEDs. IEDs can be placed in the ground like land mines, they can be worn on "suicide belts," or they can be placed in vehicles. At least half, and perhaps two-thirds, of all American combat deaths and injuries in Afghanistan and Iraq were due to IEDs. These bombs resulted in far more burns and **amputations** than previous wars. Doctors also saw many more "invisible" injuries, such as post-traumatic stress disorder (PTSD) and traumatic brain injuries (both discussed in this chapter).

Just as the Vietnam War led to improvements in emergency care, more recent wars are also leading to improvements in treating certain injuries. For example, one of the major causes of death on the battlefield is blood loss. Doctors in Afghanistan and Iraq pioneered new techniques in stopping bleeding, which allowed more soldiers to survive. Another important field of research is prosthetics, which are manmade limbs that replace those lost in war (or other accidents). Exciting developments in robotics are making it possible for soldiers who lost limbs to regain more of their physical independence. And these advances will also improve civilian health care.

## TRAUMATIC BRAIN INJURY

Just as doctors in the Vietnam War learned a lot about treating bullet wounds (see sidebar), so military doctors are learning a lot about brain injuries today. The name for these types of wounds is *traumatic brain injury* (TBI). TBI can be caused by a sudden, violent blow to the head, or by an object (such as a skull fragment) piercing the brain tissue. Both of these situations can result in hematomas (ruptured blood vessels) or contusions (bruised tissue).

TBIs can be mild, moderate, or severe. Symptoms of mild TBI include:

- headache
- confusion
- dizziness
- vision problems
- difficulty with memory or concentration
- ringing in the ears
- changes in behavior or mood

Moderate and severe TBI symptoms include all of the above, plus vomiting, nausea, seizures, slurred speech, and loss of coordination. The most serious TBIs can put the sufferer in a coma.

You certainly don't need to go to war to suffer from a TBI. Falls, car accidents, and sports injuries can also cause them. But much of our recent knowledge of TBIs comes from the large number of soldiers who were hit by IEDs in Iraq and Afghanistan. Researchers have also noticed that TBI symptoms can be found in veterans who were not directly struck by IEDs, but who were nearby when one exploded. Doctors suspect that a bomb blast creates a pressure wave that passes through the skull and causes a TBI. The U.S. Department of Defense reports that nearly a quarter of a million soldiers have experienced mild TBIs due to these "blast events."

Like PTSD, TBIs are very tough on families. Especially if the injury is severe, the veteran may not be able to contribute to the family the way he or she once did. In fact, survivors may need a lot of caregiving themselves. That puts a big burden on spouses to keep their families together. It's also hard on kids because their parent, while still alive, is not the same. It's totally normal to "grieve" for the parent you had before the injury. Even though you are grateful that your parent is still alive, it's only natural to be sad or even angry that he or she has been injured. Your "old" parent has been taken away, and you have to get used to a "new" one who may need a lot of help.

## A SENSE OF PURPOSE

In many ways, military families have more challenges to deal with than civilians do. But there are also benefits. Of course there are some of the perks mentioned earlier, such as free travel. But more importantly, military families tend

A Navy officer greets her family as she returns from a five-month deployment.

to have a larger sense of purpose. They understand that they are engaged in a something far bigger than any individual—protecting and defending their country. Because it's not just the soldier or officer who serves the country—their family does, too.

> They also serve,
> who only stand and wait.
>
> —John Milton

The armed forces often come to feel like a big, extended family. And a lot of families say that the military experience has made their family stronger, not weaker. The sense of honor and responsibility that comes with military service can bind a family even closer together.

## Text-Dependent Questions

1. What are some of the good and bad aspects of moving frequently?
2. What are the symptoms of PTSD?
3. What causes TBI?

## Research Project

Find out more about TBI. Aside from combat, what are other situations that can cause TBI? What ages of people are affected? What kinds of therapies are available to them? What should be done to prevent TBI? Write up what you've learned in a brief report to present to your class.

# FURTHER READING

## Books

Garrett, Sheryl, and Sue Hoppin. *A Family's Guide to the Military for Dummies.* Hoboken, NJ: Wiley, 2009.

Kohl, Peter. *My Dad is in the Army.* New York: PowerKids Press, 2016.

Miller, Nancy. *My Mom is in the Navy.* New York: PowerKids Press, 2016.

## Online

EBlue Star Families. *Everyone Serves: A Handbook for Family and Friends of Service Members.* http://www.everyoneservesbook.com/.

Friedman, Matthew J. "PTSD History and Overview." U.S. Department of Veterans Affairs, National Center for PTSD. http://www.ptsd.va.gov/professional/ptsd-overview/ptsd-overview.asp.

Military Brat Life. http://militarybratlife.com/.

Military Kids Connect. http://militarykidsconnect.dcoe.mil.

Military OneSource. "Marriage and Family." http://militaryonesource.mil/family-and-relationships/marriage.

## Get Help Now

**Veterans Crisis Line**

Hotline for service members and their families. You can also text at 838255 or chat on their website.

1-800-273-8255 https://www.veteranscrisisline.net

# SERIES GLOSSARY

**agencies:** departments of a government with responsibilities for specific programs.

**anxiety:** a feeling of worry or nervousness.

**biological parents:** the woman and man who create a child; they may or not raise it.

**caregiving:** helping someone with their daily activities.

**cognitive:** having to do with thinking or understanding.

**consensus:** agreement among a particular group of people.

**custody:** legal guardianship of a child.

**demographers:** people who study information about people and communities.

**depression:** severe sadness or unhappiness that does not go away easily.

**discrimination:** singling out a group for unfair treatment.

**disparity:** a noticeable difference between two things.

**diverse:** having variety; for example, "ethnically diverse" means a group of people of many different ethnicities.

**ethnicity:** a group that has a shared cultural heritage.

**extended family:** the kind of family that includes members beyond just parents and children, such as aunts, uncles, cousins, and so on.

**foster care:** raising a child (usually temporarily) that is not adopted or biologically yours.

**heir:** someone who receives another person's wealth and social position after the other person dies.

**homogenous:** a group of things that are the same.

**ideology:** a set of ideas and ways of seeing the world.

**incarceration:** being confined in prison or jail.

**inclusive:** accepting of everyone.

**informally:** not official or legal.

**institution:** an established organization, custom, or tradition.

**kinship:** family relations.

**neglect:** not caring for something correctly.

**patriarchal:** a system that is run by men and fathers.

**prejudice:** beliefs about a person or group based only on simplified and often mistaken ideas.

**prevalence:** how common a particular trait is in a group of people.

**psychological:** having to do with the mind.

**quantify:** to count or measure objectively.

**restrictions:** limits on what someone can do.

**reunification:** putting something back together.

**secular:** nonreligious.

**security:** being free from danger.

**social worker:** a person whose job is to help families or children deal with particular problems.

**socioeconomic:** relating to both social factors (such as race and ethnicity) as well as financial factors (such as class).

**sociologists:** people who study human society and how it operates.

**spectrum:** range.

**stability:** the sense that things will stay the same.

**stereotype:** a simplified idea about a type of person that is not connected to actual individuals.

**stigma:** a judgment that something is bad or shameful.

**stressor:** a situation or event that causes upset (stress).

**traumatic:** something that's very disturbing and causes long-term damage to a person.

**variable:** something that can change.

# INDEX

Page numbers in *italics* refer to photographs or tables.

## ABOUT THE AUTHOR

**H. W. Poole** is a writer and editor of books for young people, including the 13-volume set, *Mental Illnesses and Disorders: Awareness and Understanding* (Mason Crest). She created the *Horrors of History* series (Charlesbridge) and the *Ecosystems* series (Facts On File). She has also been responsible for many critically acclaimed reference books, including *Political Handbook of the World* (CQ Press) and the *Encyclopedia of Terrorism* (SAGE). She was coauthor and editor of *The History of the Internet* (ABC-CLIO), which won the 2000 American Library Association RUSA award.

## PHOTO CREDITS

*Photos are for illustrative purposes only; individuals depicted are models.*

**Cover:** Shutterstock/Forewer

**iStock:** 6 Mordorlff; 9 Den Kuvaiev; 10 EdStock; 22 Catharine Lane; 24 Mie Ahmt; 26 BraunS; 28 Tatiana Belova; 29 Eric Vega; 32 EdStock

**Library of Congress:** 20

**Wikimedia Commons:** 13 U.S. Navy; 14 U.S. Coast Guard; 16; 17 Sgt. Olan A. Owens; 18 National Archives and Records Administration; 34 U.S. Department of Defense; 37 U.S. Department of Defense; 38 U.S. Army National Guard; 42 U.S. Navy

# DRAGONS AND LOTUS BLOSSOMS

# DRAGONS AND LOTUS BLOSSOMS

## VIETNAMESE CERAMICS FROM THE BIRMINGHAM MUSEUM OF ART

BY JOHN A. STEVENSON AND DONALD A. WOOD
WITH AN ESSAY BY PHILIPPE TRUONG

BIRMINGHAM MUSEUM OF ART, BIRMINGHAM, ALABAMA
IN ASSOCIATION WITH UNIVERSITY OF WASHINGTON PRESS, SEATTLE AND LONDON

This catalogue has been published in conjunction with the exhibition *Dragons and Lotus Blossoms: Vietnamese Ceramics from the Birmingham Museum of Art,* organized by the Birmingham Museum of Art, Birmingham, Alabama, January 22–April 8, 2012.

*Dragons and Lotus Blossoms: Vietnamese Ceramics from the Birmingham Museum of Art* is supported by grants from the E. Rhodes and Leona B. Carpenter Foundation, the National Endowment for the Arts, and the J. & H. Weldon Foundation, Inc.


www.artsbma.org

First published in 2011 by the
University of Washington Press
PO Box 50096
Seattle, WA 98145-5096
www.washington.edu/uwpress

ISBN: 978-0-295-99162-7

Cataloging-in-publication information is available from the Library of Congress



Authors: John A. Stevenson; Donald A. Wood
Designed by James Edward Williams
Photography by M. Sean Pathasema

Other photo credits:
John Stevenson: p. 17 fig. 2, p. 18 fig. 3, p. 19 fig. 4
Philippe Truong: p. 26 fig. 1, 2, 4
Tran Duc Anh Son: p. 26 fig. 3

Printed and bound in China

All measurements are in inches;
Height precedes width precedes depth unless otherwise noted.

Front Cover: Cat. 23; Back Cover: Cat. 121; Frontispiece: Cat. 24

# CONTENTS

# DIRECTOR'S FOREWORD

It is a great pleasure and honor to unveil the Birmingham Museum of Art's collection of Vietnamese ceramics in the exhibition, *Dragons and Lotus Blossoms: Vietnamese Ceramics from the Birmingham Museum of Art* and the catalogue, which accompanies this exhibition. The Museum's collection includes 219 objects, one of the largest and finest such collections in North America. The history of this collection reaches back almost 40 years to a visit from Sherman Lee, then Director of the Cleveland Museum of Art.

Dr. Lee came to Birmingham in 1972 to give a lecture on Asian art. At that time he advocated the formation of a support group for Asian art, resulting in the founding in 1974 of the Birmingham Asian Art Society. Dr. Lee also encouraged the collection of Southeast Asian ceramics for the permanent collection, and in particular Vietnamese ceramics. The first gifts and purchases soon followed in 1975. A steady stream of gifts from members of the Society continued over the years resulting in a collection that provided an outstanding overview of the rich heritage of Vietnamese ceramics.

The collection received major additions in 2005 and 2007 when William M. Spencer III acquired for the Museum an important private collection of Vietnamese ceramics. The Museum was also able to purchase at this time a private library devoted to Vietnamese ceramics. When paired with the existing collection, these additions resulted in perhaps the finest collection of Vietnamese ceramics in North America. Mr. Spencer's generosity continued after his death in 2010 with additional purchases of Vietnamese ceramics made possible by his estate.

Donald A. Wood, Ph.D., Senior Curator and The Virginia and William M. Spencer III Curator of Asian Art, has been key in the development of the collection and of this exhibition and catalogue. He understood the opportunities that presented themselves—purchases from the Hoi An shipwreck, acquisition of a large private collection and strategic purchases—that have created a collection that covers the entire range of Vietnamese ceramic production. We are grateful to him for his connoisseurship and dedication to this endeavor. Our deep appreciation also goes to John Stevenson, for his essential guidance, and to Philippe Truong for their scholarship and participation in this project. I join Don Wood in expressing my deep appreciation to the Asian Art Society for their support over the years. In addition, I thank our talented staff for their constant and consistent dedication to excellence that enables the success of projects such as this.

I want to also thank the E. Rhodes and Leona B. Carpenter Foundation, the National Endowment for the Arts, and the J. & H. Weldon Foundation, Inc. for their generous support of the exhibition and catalogue. This project would not have been possible without their kind encouragement and assistance.

Finally, I extend my heartfelt gratitude to the late Bill Spencer for his generosity, curiosity about the world, passion for art and his love of this Museum. His spirit still resonates in so many ways throughout our community and this institution.

**GAIL C. ANDREWS**
The R. Hugh Daniel Director
Birmingham Musem of Art

CAT. 120

# ACKNOWLEDGMENTS

I wish to express my gratitude to John Stevenson not only for his assistance as co-curator in the organization of this exhibition and publication but also for his scholarly contributions to the catalogue. His expertise and guidance have greatly facilitated the project. I am also grateful to Philippe Truong for his kind advice and learned essay. I wish also to thank the E. Rhodes and Leona B. Carpenter Foundation, the National Endowment for the Arts and the J. & H. Weldon Foundation, Inc. for their generous support of the exhibition and catalogue. Pat Soden and Pamela Canell of the Washington University Press were also a pleasure to work with on the catalogue.

Members of the Museum staff have worked tirelessly to bring this project to fruition. Director Gail Andrews encouraged and supported the project from its inception. James Williams did his usual beautiful work in designing the catalogue, while Sean Pathesema took all of the lovely photographs. Denny Frank, Rashid Qandil, Priscilla Tapio and Daniel White patiently and cheerfully moved all of the ceramics numerous times for photography and installation. Suzanne Stephens made endless counts and lists of the collection, always with a smile. Melissa Falkner Mercurio and Mary Villadsen patiently numbered, checked and rechecked every piece in the collection. Tatum Preston tracked down numerous articles and references for the research, while Kristi Taft searched out every possible grant and funding opportunity to support the project. And, Terry Beckham provided the beautiful installation for the accompanying exhibition.

To these, and many others, my heartfelt thanks.

**DONALD A. WOOD**

Senior Curator

The Virginia and William M. Spencer III Curator of Asian Art

Birmingham Musem of Art

# DEDICATION

*Dragons and Lotus Blossoms: Vietnamese Ceramics from the Birmingham Museum of Art* is dedicated to William M. Spencer III and the Asian Art Society at the Birmingham Museum of Art. Mr. Spencer was an avid supporter of the Museum, and in particular Asian Art. His generosity made possible, in large part, the outstanding collection of Vietnamese ceramics at the Museum. The Asian Art Society at the Museum has provided the foundation on which the entire Asian art collection has been built, and had the foresight to appreciate and collect Vietnamese ceramics long before anyone else.

# CHRONOLOGY

| | |
|---|---|
| Dong Son culture | approx 2000 bce–200 ce |
| First Chinese invasions | 221–210 bce |
| Han–Viet period | 111 bce–late second century ce |
| Van Xuan kingdom | 544–602 |
| Sui– and Tang–Viet periods | 603–906 |
| Ngo dynasty | 939–965 |
| Le dynasty | 1009–1225 |
| Tran dynasty | 1225–1400 |
| Ho dynasty | 1400–1407 |
| Ming Chinese occupation | 1407–1427 |
| Later Le dynasty | 1428–1524 |
| Mac dynasty | 1527–1592 |
| Trinh Lords in the north | 1539–1787 |
| Nguyen Lords in the south | 1558–1778 |
| Tay Son dynasty | 1788–1802 |
| Nguyen dynasty | 1802–1945 |
| French colonial rule | 1859–1954 |
| Partition | 1954–1975 |
| Socialist Republic of Vietnam | 1976– |

# MAP

## VIETNAM'S EXPANSION SOUTHWARD

The Red River Valley bordering China was Vietnam's heartland. In the year 938 the Vietnamese gained independence from China and began a steady expansion southward that lasted a thousand years. The dates here indicate when various regions were incorporated into Vietnam, until it had the borders it has today. Between the eleventh and the seventeenth century, the loosely organized kingdom of Champa, with its capital first in Vijaya and then in Panduranga, was gradually assimilated. Other areas were absorbed from the Khmer (Cambodian) empire. Unlike today, much of the south was sparsely populated, and the Nguyen Lords who ruled Vietnam in the seventeenth and eighteenth centuries planted settlements of peasants and criminals in empty areas as they moved south.

CAT. 51

CAT. 26

CAT. 57

# VIETNAMESE CERAMICS, THE DEVELOPMENT OF AN ART FORM

JOHN A. STEVENSON

In the 1960s and '70s, the destinies of Vietnam and the United States became tightly intertwined. The violence of the experience has profoundly colored the way Vietnam is viewed, with most Americans seeing the country in terms of the Vietnam War (which the Vietnamese call the American War). Few people in America are aware of Vietnam's distinctive millennia-long cultural history. At the same time as they defended their independence against powerful enemies over the centuries, the Vietnamese developed subtle and sophisticated cultural traditions. These include ceramics, which form an unusually important part of Vietnam's artistic identity.

Art objects have fared badly in Vietnam; not much has survived. Few ancient items made of wood or paper or textiles have endured Vietnam's hot and humid climate. Long before the destruction of the twentieth century, architectural monuments were lost during invasions by Vietnam's neighbors, the Khmer, the Cham, and the Chinese, even the distant Mongolians. When they occupied Vietnam from 1407 to 1427, the Chinese appear to have deliberately obliterated the art and artifacts of an alien culture different from their own, removing archives and libraries and leveling palaces and temples. But ceramics—clay that has been fired to stone—have survived. They are a physical form of Vietnam's historical memory. Along with literature, poetry, and music—art forms that can exist without tangible expression—ceramics are among the most significant manifestations of Vietnam's cultural heritage to have survived the centuries.

As a result of public-works construction during the French colonial period, ancient ceramics were unearthed in the Red River Valley and Thanh Hoa in northern Vietnam, and immediately received enthusiastic scholarly attention. In 1931 the historian Victor Goloubew prophesied, "Thanh Hoa Province will become the promised land of antiquarians and collectors. Already we say 'Thanh Hoa' just as we say a 'Song' or a 'Ming,' and without any doubt there will soon be Chinese–Vietnamese vases and bowls in all the museums of Europe and America" (*Revue des Arts Asiatiques,* vol. 7, Paris, 1931, 113). But Goloubew's vision has not been fulfilled: war intervened, and many decades later few museums in the West exhibit more than a few token Vietnamese ceramics bought at recent high-profile auctions.

The Birmingham Museum of Art (BMA) is a shining exception. As early as the 1970s, members of the Asian Art Society at the BMA recognized the beauty of Vietnamese ceramics and the potential for creating a significant collection in a little known and under-appreciated field. The BMA was able to amass a core collection of fifteenth- and sixteenth-century blue-and-white export wares, modeled on the great blue-and-whites from the imperial kilns of Jingdezhen in China. Building on this civic support, the Museum bought more export wares at the rich international auctions of shipwreck ceramics that since the year 2000 have revolutionized the study of Southeast Asian ceramics. In 2010 the collection of Mr. William M. Spencer III, long time patron of the Museum and a founding member of the Asian Art Society, was bequeathed to the Museum. This collection was particularly strong in Vietnamese ceramics made for domestic use and never exported, a neglected area in which it has been difficult to find material. The selection has been admirable, with many fine, undamaged, and unique examples entering the Museum's collection. The result is that, along with The Museum of Fine Arts in Boston, and The Metropolitan Museum of Art in New York City, the Birmingham Museum of Art now has one of the three finest collections of Vietnamese ceramics in North America.

## CONTEXT

Vietnam's modern borders are the result of an "advance southward" by the Vietnamese people beginning about a thousand years ago from their heartland in the Red River Valley, located in the north of the country bordering on China. The ceramics you see in this book were almost all produced in the Red River Valley and Thanh Hoa Province just to the south. Potters were fortunate in the very high quality of the clay deposits available there. Fine, smooth, gray-white, and homogenous, these clays could be worked into light, elegant, thin-walled vessels with complex shapes and molded and appliquéd decorations. These contrast with the clays of nearby Thailand, for example, most of which were coarse and dark, containing grit and impurities that limited the decoration and the shapes that it was possible to create. Vietnamese ceramics are stoneware; deposits of porcelain clay, which was added to kaolin in the manufacture of porcelain in China, were not available in Vietnam. Vietnamese kilns could easily produce temperatures of 1200 degrees and more—the temperature required for porcelain—but although highly fired Vietnamese ceramics often ring like porcelain, they are not translucent and not true porcelain.

Vietnamese ceramics are inevitably compared with those of China, Vietnam's giant neighbor, with its ancient manufacturing techniques and vast output, and the similarities and differences between them are major themes of this essay and the exhibition. The relationship between the two nations has long been troubled. The Chinese invaded Vietnam in 111 BCE and nominally incorporated the Red River Valley into the Han Empire. Following violent rebellions—the first of many—northern Vietnam was administered directly by Chinese generals and landowning families from about 40 CE onward. Control of northern Vietnam by the Chinese remained tenuous and intermittent for a thousand years. Chinese censuses of the first century CE show that the population of the Red River Valley was much greater—more than double—than the combined population of the larger neighboring provinces of southern China. This obliged the Chinese to try to reinstate their rule, at great cost in effort and resources, every time the fiercely independent Vietnamese forced them out of the Red River Valley. By the tenth century, after a millennium of various degrees of Chinese control of northern Vietnam, Chinese immigration into their southern provinces provided a sufficient counterweight to the large and vibrant population of the Red River Valley, so that China's strategic need to dominate Vietnam became less essential. After the disintegration of the Tang dynasty in China, the Vietnamese defeated a Chinese army sent against them in 938, and even nominal Chinese control of Vietnam ended. Except for the period of twenty years early in the fifteenth century mentioned above, the Chinese never again ruled Vietnam.

China's cultural influence was immense, yet China did not succeed in sinifying the Vietnamese. Fundamental cultural differences remained, such as a much higher status for women in Vietnam, together with non-Confucian religious ceremonies that emphasized fertility rather than ancestors. Above all, Vietnamese resistance to speaking Chinese was never overcome, so that whatever the Chinese did in Vietnam was conditioned by the filter of a different language, and thus of a different culture. At the same time, the neighboring Khmer and Cham civilizations provided the Vietnamese with cultural and intellectual alternatives to China.

This had a direct influence on ceramics. Vietnamese ceramics were at their most creative and distinctive from the eleventh to the late fifteenth century, when Vietnam was exploring its national identity after a millennium of Chinese domination. Under two native-Vietnamese dynasties, the Ly (1009–1225) and the Tran (1225–1400), original shapes and types of ceramics, along with local decorative motifs, were developed in a riot of experimentation. Ceramics from these four hundred years form the heart of the collection presented in this book. The Chinese themselves valued ceramics made in Vietnam. The *Yuanshi*, Yuan dynastic history, records an edict of 1262 in which the Shizu emperor, the Mongolian Kublai Khan, defined the form of goods that he expected a Vietnamese prince to supply the following year: besides the usual tropical luxury items, such as pearls and rhinoceros horn, he requested white ceramic bowls. When the Chinese developed underglaze cobalt-blue-painted dishes and vessels in the fourteenth century, the Vietnamese produced their own fine versions—and when the Chinese looked inwards, banning exports, Vietnam filled the vacuum, shipping blue-and-white wares of extraordinarily high quality to Islamic markets from Indonesia to Persia and Turkey. Ornate, almost baroque, forms of incense-burners and candleholders were then developed for Buddhist monasteries. But after the sixteenth century the quality of Vietnamese ceramic production declined.

## THE EVOLUTION OF VIETNAMESE CERAMICS

Southeast Asia is home to some of the oldest ceramics in the world. The Vietnamese trace their ceramic culture back at least six thousand years, to the Hoa Binh–Bac Son culture of northern Vietnam. A primitive wheel was used as early as the Phung Nguyen culture, four thousand years ago. The various peoples who lived in the Red River Valley produced a variety of ceramics decorated by stamping, impressing, engraving, combing, and incising. The earliest glazed wares date to the Han–Viet period (111 BCE to late second century CE)—two millennia ago—when China controlled the Red River Valley. Sophisticated shapes following Chinese bronze vessels (cat. 7) were given a thin whitish glaze, sometimes with thick decorative glassy-green glaze splashes deliberately applied. Vietnamese ceramics from the third to the tenth century, following the Han–Viet period, are rather primitive; most are heavy and undecorated, and no distinctive Vietnamese ceramic style appears to have developed during this time.

In 1009 a native clan, the Ly, gained control of northern Vietnam with the help of the Buddhist establishment. Naming their kingdom Dai Viet, they settled their capital on the site of what is now Hanoi. They called the city Thang Long, "Rising Dragon"; the Vietnamese believe they are descended from dragons, and dragons became beloved and very common decorative motifs on ceramics of all sorts, from bricks for the palace to beakers and ewers. Vietnamese culture flowered under the Ly as Vietnamese explored their identity independent of China. Potters incorporated indigenous Vietnamese themes while absorbing artistic characteristics from neighboring cultures, and from metal and stone artifacts besides ceramics. China was the strongest influence, not just because China was Vietnam's most powerful neighbor but because of the overwhelming beauty and sophistication of China's ceramic tradition. Yet even when using Chinese prototypes, the potters of Ly and Tran did not usually copy them directly. They would take shapes, glazes, and decorative motifs and use them in original ways.

For example, a popular Song Chinese motif celebrates fertility and abundance by depicting young boys playing among peony flowers. The theme is common on Song white and light-blue monochromes, whereas in Vietnam the motif is associated with darker glazes (cats. 51, 53).

FIG. 1
CAT. 58
Bowl with green glaze and strongly inverted sides, lotus flowers and arrowhead plants carved on the interior, floral design in well, 13th–14th century

An ivory-yellow bowl might have molded dragons on the inner sides and a chrysanthemum in the well (cat. 27): Chinese potters would have combined dragons with waves or clouds, never a flower. Vietnamese dragons themselves are different from Chinese dragons, longer and more sinuous (cat. 10).

Besides motifs, Ly and Tran potters developed unique ceramic shapes. Bowls with wavy-edged lotus-leaf covers are among the most elegant (cat. 57)—their silhouette is broader and they are thinner-walled than their Chinese Longquan equivalents. The iron-based green glaze of the Vietnamese was clear and glassy—jewel-like—where Longquan celadon glaze was opaque, filled with tiny bubbles—jade-like. Other uniquely Vietnamese shapes include beakers and bowls with straight or gently curving sides (cats. 38, 63, 65) and bowls with elegantly inverted rims and finely carved interiors (fig. 1, cat. 58). The sharply inverted and shapely profiles of the latter were hardly seen in China; indeed, the shapes of Vietnamese ceramics generally during the four hundred years of Ly and Tran are pregnant and robust, with no hint of the attenuation or over-refinement of some Song and Yuan shapes. It would have been easy for potters to make direct copies of Chinese products, as happened during the Han–Viet period. That they did not do so argues against theories that expatriate Chinese potters, working in Vietnam for economic or political reasons, were responsible for the ceramic innovations of Ly and Tran.

The Vietnamese also developed their own production techniques. Perhaps the most significant was a brown inlay used against an ivory background, a glazing method used in Vietnam to decorate many larger shapes, especially tall cylindrical storage jars (cats. 17, 18, 19). A low-iron-content wood-ash glaze (perhaps two percent iron) was applied to the body of the vessel and a design created by scraping away some of the still-viscous glaze before it dried. An ash glaze with a much higher iron content (perhaps six percent) was applied to the scraped areas. The high-iron glaze would fire to a dark chocolate brown that contrasted pleasingly with the ivory-white background. Superficially the effect was similar to Chinese *Cizhou* wares, where a chocolate-brown design was painted on a light-colored clay body or applied white slip, and the whole covered with a clear transparent glaze before firing. It is possible that Vietnamese potters developed the new technique because they could not always control the transparency of an overall glaze (fig. 2), whereas inlay in a carved-away design would always show up against the background.

Bowl with slightly inverted sides, incised lotus-petal design on exterior, row of bosses emulating drum-skin nails below the rim, chocolate-painted base with chocolate-brown wash over body under partially opaque ivory-yellow glaze, probably intended to be clear, 13th–14th century (private collection). FIG. 2

Other more rounded jars, both tall and small, were decorated around the shoulder and on the cover with a frieze of carved lotus petals, the most ubiquitous decorative motif on Ly and Tran ceramics. The exteriors of another uniquely Vietnamese shape, offering dishes used perhaps on altars (cats. 11, 12), were made up of lotus petals, carved individually. The lotus flower, which grows in water and emerges unsullied from the mud, is the archetypal symbol of Buddhist purity throughout South and Southeast Asia. Lotus flowers were incised, carved, and molded on a vast range of Vietnamese bowls, dishes, and ewers, reflecting both the fondness of the Vietnamese for decorative motifs taken from nature and the profound influence of the Buddhist monkhood. Vietnam was a strongly Buddhist society at this time, and the Buddhist establishment was extremely powerful during both the Ly and Tran dynasties—court edicts expressed concern at the political influence of Buddhist monasteries and how resources and potential taxes were diverted when large numbers of young people became spiritually potent but economically unproductive monks and nuns. Some of the many Vietnamese vessels of all sorts decorated with lotus flowers or petals would have been used in temples and monasteries, others by wealthier lay people on domestic altars. Today we are so used to glazed vessels that it is worth remembering that most ceramics for daily use would have been simple and unglazed, and that the labor required for any glazed or decorated ceramics made them objects of some value.

The skill of Vietnamese potters is evident in a unique group of large ewers in the Birmingham Collection (cats. 23, 24, 25). They are marvelously light, with finely made decorative spouts, handles, and lids, and applied designs. Their forms suggest metal prototypes, which are not easily transposed into ceramics. Full and imposing, these ewers are not found in the repertoire of Chinese shapes, and non-Chinese features appear in their decoration. For example, the spouts take the form of animal heads, one a gilled *makara* (a mythical aquatic beast from India combining features of a crocodile and an elephant), another a *garuda* (the birdlike vehicle of the Hindu deity Vishnu), together with a Vietnamese dragon. A related ewer (cat. 26) has a long-nosed *makara* spout, also with aquatic gills. Two of the ewer covers are lobed like a lotus-leaf, and one has a small frieze of spiky lotus petals. The perfection of the potting and the lightness and thinness of the walls of these ewers are extraordinary. With their dragon (royal) motifs, perhaps they were made for the court. Other examples of such thin-walled lightness in Birmingham's collection from this period include beakers and bowls (cats. 38, 39).

## EXPORT WARES

Vietnamese ceramics were traded to the mountain tribes south and west of the northern Vietnamese heartland, as far as Thailand and Burma, and have been found in large quantities in medieval mountain-tribe burial sites. They have been found in even greater numbers at burial sites in the Philippines and Indonesia, from small monochrome bowls with lotus-petal rims to larger vessels, including glassy-green celadons. Vietnamese ceramics have also been found in small quantities in Japanese habitation and temple sites; for example, shards of Vietnamese bowls with underglaze iron-brown decoration similar to the daisy-like motif of catalogue 112 have been unearthed at Kanzeon temple in the ancient port-city of Dazaifu in western Japan. These fragments are important, as their archaeological contexts date them to the first half of the fourteenth century, the same time as painted underglaze decoration was being developed in China.

When Chinese potters mastered the use of cobalt-blue pigments for underglaze decoration, the Vietnamese quickly adopted the more attractive blue color for the previously iron-brown daisy/chrysanthemum motifs that had already found acceptance in export markets. When the imperial factories in China produced blue-and-white vessels for export to the Muslim world, Vietnamese potters were motivated to do the same. Most Vietnamese blue-and-whites were made for export, not domestic use. Bottles, jars, and large dishes suited to Muslim tastes found markets from Indonesia to Egypt; examples have been treasured in collections in Turkey and Iran for centuries. A documented jar now in Dresden reached Europe, and in 1590 was given to the Elector of Saxony. Other shapes satisfied specialized markets, for example, *kendi* water sprinklers and large wall tiles were made in Vietnam specifically for the Indonesian market. Distinctly Vietnamese design motifs, especially fish and dragons, peonies and lotuses, were created to decorate large dishes. The best examples of Vietnamese underglaze-blue painting are full of vigor and imagination that surpass formal Chinese interpretations of similar themes. Simpler examples often have a sense of playfulness, especially in representations of animals, mythical and real. As an example of the whimsicality of Vietnamese potters, figure 3 shows a playful little sketch of a *chich chòe* bird, the equivalent of a sparrow in the West.

Painting techniques were refined further, with overglaze colored enamels—red, green, and sometimes yellow—augmenting the blue-on-white background. These colored enamels were applied to the surface of a fired piece, which was then fired a second time at lower temperatures. Vietnamese potters developed idiosyncratic designs for these three- and four-color wares, including landscapes, large birds, and real and mythical animals, some of which are very lively and imaginative. A unique example is the large painted jar in the Birmingham Collection (cat. 121) that may be the most elaborately decorated example of Vietnamese multicolored painting in any collection anywhere. The finest Vietnamese underglaze-blue pieces date from the fourteenth and fifteenth centuries, and the finest overglaze enameled wares from the late fifteenth and early sixteenth centuries.

In the last two decades we have learned much about these highly vigorous and sophisticated painted Vietnamese pieces from the recovery of material from shipwrecks in Southeast Asian waters. Perhaps the most significant has been the shipwreck off Hoi An, near Danang, where a quarter of a million ceramics have been raised from the sea-bed, with hundreds of thousands more left in the wreck, attesting to the very large scale of the ceramics trade. In this case, the ship was probably grossly overloaded, and sank only a few miles after it headed out to sea. A shipwreck is a time capsule: a vast range of ceramics of different shapes and forms of decoration were being carried in the Hoi An vessel, demonstrating that, contrary to previous thinking, pieces of many different shapes and types of decoration were being made simultaneously.

A feature of many large export wares and other, smaller pieces that never left Vietnam is the application of a brown pigment to the base, sometimes described as a "chocolate wash." So common are chocolate-washed

FIG. 3 Base of small dish, cobalt-blue decoration on white-slipped body, partial chocolate-wash to base with playful sketch of *chich chòe* bird, 16th century (private collection).

FIG. 4 Small incense-burner, Chinese, painted cobalt-blue floral design, chocolate wash on base, 15th–16th century (private collection).

FIG. 5 Base of green-glazed covered bowl, 13th–14th century, with brown daub, a potter's mark or perhaps a precursor of chocolate-washed bases (private collection)

FIG. 6 Base of large Chinese celadon dish showing the change of color to the unglazed clay that results from reduction firing, 15th century (private collection).

bases on Vietnamese ceramics of the fourteenth through sixteenth centuries that they are a useful indicator that a piece is Vietnamese. Their purpose has been much discussed and many theories suggested (the author was in correspondence about them with Roxanna Brown at the time of her outrageous death). Among the earliest theories was that of d'Argencé, who believed their purpose was religious. Such an intentional chocolate-brown wash was rare in Chinese ceramics but not unknown (fig. 4). A brown daub on the base of a Vietnamese covered green-glazed bowl, very similar to cat. 57, may be a precursor of this wash (fig. 5). Also, a thin brown often appears on the unglazed bases of Longquan celadons, the result of firing in reduced kiln conditions to produce the green glaze (fig. 6). High-quality Longquan bowls and dishes imported from China have been unearthed in Vietnam in fairly large numbers, and this writer believes that the Vietnamese chocolate wash may have been simply an aesthetic touch, made to complete a ceramic visually, possibly copying Chinese examples admired by Vietnamese potters and consumers.

## DECLINE

The finest Vietnamese underglaze-blue pieces date from the fourteenth and fifteenth centuries, and the finest over-glaze enameled wares from the late fifteenth and early sixteenth centuries. During this time the Chinese Ming government discouraged exports, especially during the years 1436 to 1465, leaving markets open to Vietnamese exploitation. The Vietnamese expulsion of Ming armies from Hanoi in 1427 inaugurated a period of prosperity and peace, culminating in the reign of Le Thanh Tong (1468–1490). By the beginning of the sixteenth century, however, peasant rebellions and attempted coups by ambitious members of the royal clan had brought chaos to the country.

Civil war plagued Vietnam for the rest of the sixteenth century—and the quality of Vietnamese ceramics tended to decline. When China reversed restrictions on its export trade, Vietnam was squeezed out of international ceramics markets by good-quality mass-produced Chinese wares. Against a background of unrest and instability, Vietnamese ceramics lost their simple focus and self-confidence. Production became rough and careless. The most interesting innovations during the sixteenth and seventeenth centuries were large and imposing items of altar furniture such as candle-stands and incense-burners (cat. 165), commissioned by Buddhist temples, but their shapes are overly complex and the refinement of form of earlier wares was lost. Fanciful types of the distinctive Vietnamese lime-pots, paraphernalia for betelnut chewing, were popular (cat. 153). Underglaze-cobalt painting was usually vigorous but often crude (cat. 166).

The export of ceramics revived for a time during the second half of the seventeenth century, when the Dutch East India Company shipped low-quality Vietnamese wares to Batavia in Indonesia by the millions. The ceramics industry declined precipitously when in the eighteenth century the Nguyen and Trinh governments imposed their own trade restrictions. The long-established export kilns at Chu Dau apparently ceased production at this time, though Bat Trang, supported by the domestic market, continued as an important production center and remains so today.

## AESTHETICS

Alongside the importance of ceramics for an understanding of Vietnamese history and culture comes a simple appreciation of their beauty. The best Vietnamese ceramics are untrammeled, combining a lack of restraint with great potting skills. They have an attractive informality, like Korean ceramics. Yanagi Soetsu, father of the Mingei movement in Japan, was awed by the beauty achieved so easily by Korean potters. They would casually set up their wheels and not care if the results were slightly out of true. Imperfections gave great vigor to their work, yet could not be calculated without destroying their spontaneity. It is the interface between art and technology that gives ceramics their flavor. The Chinese potter aimed for perfect technique, characterized by the colossal and almost mechanistic production of the great kilns at Longquan and Jingdezhen. The Japanese potter responded to the beauty of kiln accidents, which were sometimes carefully orchestrated, a paradox. The unassuming Vietnamese ceramic tradition falls somewhere in between.

Such serendipitous combination of spontaneity with technical excellence makes Vietnamese ceramics very attractive. The bowl of figure 2 is beautifully made;

CAT. 78

it is thin-walled, wide, with a row of bosses imitating drum-skin nails under the rim, and an elegant slightly inverted silhouette. The potter has applied a dark chocolate-brown glaze over the body and rapidly incised a loose frieze of lotus petals to show through the brown, only to have this decoration almost obscured by an ivory over-glaze. The glaze must have been formulated with the expectation that it would be transparent, yet the unintended result is a subtle, complex, original, and unique work of art.

A more tactile example of ceramic aesthetics is the bulbous ewer (cat. 104), a distinctive Vietnamese type of the Tran dynasty. Its distinctive shape, with round pregnant body, dish-mouth, narrow neck, and decorative handle, is pleasing, and the forming and luting together of the several elements is skilful. The piece would have functioned successfully as a vessel for wine or water and, the shape fitting beautifully in the hands, would have been a pleasure to hold. (With the handle decorative rather than functional, both hands, one on each side of the body, would have been used for pouring.) The application of slip and clear over-glaze is casual, and the loosely floral underglaze-iron decoration has been applied with speed and abandon. Adding to the sense of informality is the natural melting of the glaze, which has collected in drips around the base. Again, the qualities achieved by such a relaxed approach cannot be controlled. Contrasting the perfection of Chinese products with the freedom and individuality of this sort of piece, a Vietnamese ceramics scholar (whose father, the head of the Hue Museum, was killed during the Tet offensive of 1969) has said, "Chinese ceramics are good for the eye; Vietnamese ceramics are good for the heart."

# VIETNAMESE CERAMICS, THE STATE OF THE FIELD

PHILIPPE TRUONG

For decades, Vietnam was preoccupied with war and recovery from war. Following the nation's opening to the wider world in the late 1980s, the country's history and culture has received more intensive international study and attention. In the field of ceramics, this has led to the publication of a number of books in English, Japanese, German, and other languages, making the subject accessible to international scholars and collectors. Very substantial quantities of shipwreck material have been discovered and sold at auction, firing international interest including the interest of major art museums around the world. In the present decade the state of the field is focused on three connected activities: academic study and archaeological work, including shipwrecks, the activity of forgers, and the interest of collectors. This essay will discuss all three.

## MUSEUM ACTIVITY

Since 1975, archaeological research and excavations have been under the control of the Vietnamese Institute of Archaeology, the only organization able to authorize and undertake actions. Other central institutions such as the Department of History of the University of Hanoi, the Archaeological Section of the University of Social Sciences (Ho Chi Minh City), the National Museum of Vietnamese History (Hanoi) and the Museum of Vietnamese History (Ho Chi Minh City) participate in this work, also the archaeologists based in provincial museums, though to a lesser extent. Discoveries are studied and dated by the Institute of Archaeology before they are published. The most special objects discovered enrich the collections of the National Museum of Vietnamese History in Hanoi and Ho Chi Minh City, while others are given back to the provincial museums where the objects have been excavated. Thanks to the actions of the Vietnamese Institute of Archaeology, a continuous line of development from the early Stone Age to today has been established, permitting us to understand the evolution of Vietnamese art.

Next to the provincial and city museums and, more rarely, the private museums, the national museums depend on the Ministry of Culture and Information; the two main national museums are the National Vietnamese History Museum of Hanoi and the Vietnamese History Museum of Ho Chi Minh City. As their names indicate, their purpose is to relate and popularize the history of Vietnam since prehistory to the present day, through historical and art objects, documents, and photographs. This is the work of three departments: "Exhibition & Propaganda" (which also organizes temporary exhibitions), "Research & Collection," and "Inventory and Preservation" (which is responsible for collection, storage, and preservation). The "Research & Collection" Department maintains and studies the collection of the museum and helps to examine artifacts from local museums, historical sites (pagodas, communal houses, temples) and participates in their protection and restoration. It also contributes to the discoveries and excavations of the archaeological sites and submarine archaeological activities, in collaboration with its own experts and international organizations.

## SHIPWRECKS

Between 1990 and 2002 five shipwrecks were identified and excavated off the coast of Vietnam. They include wrecks at Hon Cau Island (Ba Ria, Vung Tau Province, excavated between 1990 to 1991); Hon Dam Island (Kien Giang Province, 1991); Cu Lao Cham Island (Quang Nam Province, 1997 to 1999); Ca Mau (Ca Mau Province, 1998 to 1999); and Binh Thuan (Binh Thuan Province, 2001 to 2002). Except for the Cu Lao Cham shipwreck, all the cargoes contained Chinese porcelains and Thai ceramics. The Hon Cau shipwreck yielded more than 60,000 objects, mostly Kangxi porcelains, of which 28,000 were sold at auction in Amsterdam by Christie's in 1992. The Hon Dam shipwreck contained about 16,000 Thai brown and celadon wares from the Sawankhalok kilns of the fifteenth century. The Binh Thuan boat transported over 60,000 Wanli blue-and-white and polychrome ceramics produced in southern Chinese kilns (Zhangzhou and Guangzhou). Regarding the Ca Mau shipwreck, 60,000 Yongzheng porcelains were excavated officially and formed part of a sale at Sotheby's in the Netherlands in 2007, but double that number were illegally recovered by fishermen and traded inside and outside Vietnam.

Retrieving antiquities become a second activity for some fishermen from Binh Thuan Province in Central Vietnam to Ca Mau in South Vietnam, a process that has recently revealed new shipwrecks off the coast of Kien Giang and Ca Mau Provinces. Cargos contained Chinese porcelains and Thai ceramics dating from the fourteenth and fifteenth centuries. Yuan and Thai celadons that have just appeared on the Ho Chi Minh City market come from a new shipwreck off the coast of Phu Quoc Island.

The presence of Vietnamese ceramics among Chinese and Thai wares in shipwrecks off the coast of Southeast Asian islands has confirmed the dating of these finds. Included are blue-and-white ceramics decorated with chrysanthemums and clouds from the fourteenth century (from the Rang Kwian shipwreck, Thailand, 1976, and Turiang, Malaysia); blue-and-white fifteenth-century ceramics from the Chu Dau kilns (Lena junk, Philippines, 1997); Binh Dinh ceramics, produced at Go Sanh or Truong Cuu, dating from the fifteenth century (Pandanang, Philippines, 1993 to 1995).

The most important discovery of Vietnamese export ceramics has been the Cu Lao Cham shipwreck, excavated between May 1997 and June 1999 and yielding more than 240,000 artifacts (some of which were sold at auction by Butterfields of San Francisco in 2000). Dated from the late fifteenth to early sixteenth centuries, these items were produced at the Chu Dau kilns (Hai Duong Province) and kilns in Thang Long (Hanoi). Such a great range of forms, décors, and glaze types had never been found before, casting light on many questions related to the study of Vietnamese ceramics. With this find, many new shapes and forms of decoration appeared for the first time. Some decorations demonstrate that Vietnamese potters took special orders for the Southeast Asian markets. Beside celadons and the classic brown and cobalt painting, there are items with cobalt combined with polychrome painting (sometimes gilding on luxury vessels), and blue, gray-blue, and green-gray glazes.

Hoi An fishermen recovered ceramics from this cargo and sold them on to antique dealers before 1997. Some who did not know good cleaning techniques placed these items in a Javel bath or in a solution of sulphuric acid and water that damaged the glaze. After such treatments, the glaze becomes slightly scratchy and sticky. Some damaged artifacts lost all or part of their polychrome decoration. Potters repainted them, then fired them at low temperatures. Regarding the Chu Dau decorative techniques of the fifteenth century, cobalt blue was used by the master potter to draw the main decoration with thick or fine brushes before firing at high temperatures. Red enamel was then applied with fine brushes and green enamel, mostly dots, with thick brushes. Then the piece was fired a second time at low temperatures, and, finally gold might be added to the most luxurious vessels. After exposure to saltwater, the blue cobalt survived well but the colored enamels were eroded, first gold was dameged, then red, then green enamels. Sometime details deteriorated completely and are visible only as "ghost lines." The original red color varies from maroon to reddish orange. This information allows us to distinguish repainted artifacts, where the glaze is too shiny and the red enamel too bright.

## FORGERIES

It is necessary to differentiate copies and forgeries. A forgery is a fake piece produced with the commercial purpose of deceiving collectors and buyers.

The fascination of ancient Vietnamese potters with Chinese ceramics was so strong that the production of Chinese prototypes continued for a very long time. For example, Han styles continued to be used until the tenth century and Song styles until the fifteenth century, during the early Lê dynasty. These pieces pay homage to the brilliant civilization to the North. There is no proof that forgeries were produced in Vietnam before the second half of the nineteenth century when Chinese merchants settled in the country and ordered the first reproductions in the style of Trinh porcelains. For this reason, the forgery of "Hue Blue," bleu de Hue, is a good way to understand this process. Bleu de Hue is the name given by the French to Chinese porcelains ordered by Vietnamese and produced to specific Vietnamese designs. This tradition continued till the eighteenth century when the Trinh lords (1545–1786) who governed North Vietnam under the name of the Lê kings, placed orders in China for blue-and-white porcelains for use in their residences at Thang Long (now Hanoi). These items have their own decorations and marks. At the end of the Trinh government in 1786 these ceramics were seized by the new king Quang Trung (1789–1792) and their reproduction was no longer prohibited. A Bat Trang potter attempted to copy them in stoneware, as demonstrated by a plate decorated with two elephants by a banana tree and the mark *noi phu thi trung* (inner residence). This is basically an homage because the decoration is not in Trinh style.

During the Nguyen dynasty (1802–1945), dignitaries and rich landowners collected Trinh porcelains. Facing increased demand and a rarity of pieces, Chinese merchants who had settled in Vietnam ordered reproductions in China for the first time. These are present in collections made before 1975, such as the Duong Minh Thoi, Ho Dinh, Vuong Hong Sen, and Co Trung Nguon Collections. We can distinguish three types. The first consists of quite faithful copies of Trinh decoration such as two dragons and a flaming pearl on the *noi phu thi trung* plates in the style of Trinh Giang (1729–1740) and Trinh Sam (1767–1782), or the two crabs and lotus of the *noi phu thi nam* (enclosure of the south) productions. This last decoration is not painted as exquisitely as the original and, sometimes, Chinese potters forgot to reproduce decoration on the exterior or the Trinh mark, *noi phu thi nam*. The nineteenth-century dragons lack the nervous and agitated movements they exhibit on the Trinh plates, with the arrangement losing its perfect symmetry; also, the dragons' features were sometimes borrowed from Nguyen-style pieces. A second type of collection featured porcelains with new forms of decoration mixing Trinh elements of ornamentation, as on a Vuong Hong Sen bowl with a four-clawed dragon and a kylan with a flaming pearl. The painting is stereotyped, the animal's features rough, and the two shades of cobalt regular.

A third and last type, produced in South China, is different from the previous two. These pieces borrowed two Trinh marks, *noi phu thi trung* and *noi phu thi huu* (enclosure of the center), but their ornamentation

FIG. 1 Copy of *Noi Phu Thi Trung* bleu de Hue by a potter of Bat Trang during the Quang Trung reign (1753–1792).

FIG. 2 Chinese fake of *Noi Phu Thi Huu* bleu de Hue showing a typical Chinese landscape (19th century).

FIG. 3 Covered footed bowl ordered in China by Emperor Thieu Tri (1841-1847) for his own table service.

FIG. 4 Dish with *noi phu thi nam* mark on base, Canh Hung period (1740–1789)

is characteristic of Chinese styles of the nineteenth century, such as dragons pursuing pearls among clouds as decoration on bottles, landscapes with an "apple tree," or the Four Fine Arts of Chinese tradition (music, chess, calligraphy, and painting) on tea services, and Kangxi-type decoration with a dragon and a heavenly horse between the sun and moon on bowls. Incontestably, these items are forgeries but they were intended for different recipients: the two first types of better quality with quite faithful Trinh decorations or new forms of decoration in Trinh style were intended for connoisseurs (dignitaries and wealthy collectors), while the third was aimed at the nouveaux riches. During the second half of the nineteenth century, Chinese merchants also ordered copies of Nguyen porcelains with the marks Ming Mang and Thieu Tri with dragon designs; these types are easily recognizable thanks to the badly depicted dragons.

A second period of forgeries started in the 1990s when Vietnamese dealers ordered fake bleu de Hue in China. A passion for bleu de Hue was unleashed with the publication of books dedicated to the subject (*Porcelain Qing,* Beurdeley and Raindre, 1986, with a chapter on bleu de Hue based on the Co Trung Nguon Collection; *Khao ve do su co men lam Hue (A Study of Bleu de Hue)* by Vuong Hong Sen, 1993); etc. It was fanned by the debate between Tran Dinh Son and Pham Hy Tung through press articles and auction sales in France (Co Trung Nguon, November 1990; Prince Bao Long, November 1995; Ho Dinh, December 1996; etc). Within a few years, the price of bleu de Hue rocketed. For example, a quite common *noi phu thi trung* plate with two dragon-decoration (diameter 9 cm) cost 1,000 francs at the Co Trung Nguon sale of 1990, and 3500 francs at the Ho Dinh sale of 1996. A rare *noi phu thi huu* bowl with dragon and phoenix (diameter 19.5 cm) sold for 8,000 francs in 1990 and 39,000 francs six years later.

Such bidding up of prices and the paucity of pieces encouraged Ho Chi Minh antique dealers to order fake pieces in southern China. At first, Chinese potters were satisfied to copy existing decoration, using published images as models. This did not permit them to reproduce originals faithfully. A good example of this period is a forged *Trinh Sam noi phu thi trung* plate with a landscape showing a lady sitting behind a table in a garden surrounded by two maids. In the original, the drawing is very refined and nicely executed, showing a ruyi scepter and a peach branch on the table, indicating a wish for longevity. This plate in a private Paris collection was published for the first time in 1995. Two years later there appeared a copy with poor and stylized painting in which the same decoration displays a modern table and a lady holding the ruyi in her hand, without any symbolic wish. In a second example, the dealer mixed Trinh designs together on a bowl with the mark *khanh xuan thi ta* (eternal spring, enclosure of the left) and a dragon and kylan paying homage to a flaming pearl. Such ornamentation is never present on Trinh pieces. We must remember that the *khanh xuan thi ta* was a cultural vessel so that the central design always bears the two characters *khanh tho* (celebrate longevity). Finally, dealers ordered new decorations, especially with the mark *noi phu thi doai* (inner palace, enclosure of the west), such as one with a landscape in willow-pattern style including a man in a house in front of a lotus pond, or two ladies in front of a pond, or a man sitting holding a Chinese hat and a servant behind him. One dealer privately confirmed these pieces to be fakes. In 2001, the same dealer ordered excellent copies at Jingdezhen that are not easily recognized, using an authentic item as model. The only perceptible difference is the reign mark.

Unfortunately, fakes are not limited to bleu de Hue: all Vietnamese artifacts (bronzes, ceramics, wooden or stone statues, etc.) are now copied. During recent years, many forgery centers have been closed down by the police at Hoa Lu, Hanoi, Me Linh and in Thanh Hoa and Quang Ninh Provinces. Since 1990, Bat Trang potters have persisted in producing ceramics in the styles of the fifteenth and sixteenth centuries. These pieces are more reproductions than forgeries, even though some dealers sell them as authentic pieces. It is very easy to recognize these reproductions, particularly pieces from the 1990s that have thick glaze and pale-colored painting.

From 1995, fake ceramics were produced imitating an authentic piece or creating a new form or decoration from an original model. For example, from the Cu Lao Cham shipwreck appeared a rare anthropomorphic ewer in the form of a Chinese man holding a ewer. A Vietnamese potter produced a forgery, indicated by certain unlikely features such as the presence of a Western-style collar instead of a traditional wrap collar, the unusual shape of the ewer, and the closed eyes that are unprecedented in Vietnamese ceramics.

Moreover, the chocolate glaze that covers the hat on the fake pieces is similar to the chocolate base composed of a mixture of potassium permanganate and water. The artificial method of aging these objects is to expose them to rain and sun or to rub the unglazed base with a rusty knife. These techniques are easily recognizable.

Some years later, a Hanoi potter produced items with attractive new forms and decorations. He borrowed the forms from well known Yuan and Ming pieces mostly in the Sir Percival David Foundation, London. The items he produced were generally large (height: 50 to 60 cm), enlarging existing small-sized pieces from the Cu Lao Cham shipwreck, or mixing polychrome painting with molded designs in high relief (fishes, dragons) in the Bat Trang or Hai Duong styles.

In the last ten years, fakes have become more perfected. Potters reduce earthenware potsherds to powder, then use the material to reproduce forged Han house models or Han- and Ly- or Tran-style ceramics. Fortunately, they are not always satisfied to reproduce an original form but invent new ones. So when confronted by a peculiar shape, collectors must use their judgment and abstain from buying. Originality is not a virtue of present-day Vietnamese potters. They prefer the simple and the sober, with natural realism in the decoration and always with a symbolist reference. These productions reflect perfectly the image and the mentality of their creators.

Two other features permitting us to discern fakes are the presence of small air bubbles in the glaze and when the paste looks like bisque, proving that these items were purified mechanically and fired with gas rather than wood.

## COLLECTING

The abundance of the forgeries eventually raised suspicions and destroyed the confidence of collectors. After the vogue for Vietnamese ceramics in the West between 1995 and 2000, collectors began to turn away. Some sold their pieces, reducing prices on the market. Collecting at present is left to some amateurs and foreigners of Vietnamese origin who continue to buy.

Until the mid-1990s the prices of Vietnamese ceramics within Vietnam were very low, for three main reasons: the small number of collectors, their preference for porcelain rather than ceramics, and the abundance of such pieces as a result of illegal excavations. Despite the prohibition of the export of antiquities, most were bought and sent outside the country. Collectors in North Vietnam around this time tended to be interested in Vietnamese ceramics while the collectors in the South, following Vuong Hong Sen, Tran Dinh Son, and Pham Hy Tung, prefered bleu de Hue. The last two were not enthusiasts but researchers with little motive to increase the value of their pieces. From 1994 to 1996, they published more than twenty articles and books between them, contributing to the study of bleu de Hue. The researches of Tran Duc Anh Son, the former curator of Hue Museum, were also of great value.

With the economic development of the country, many successful Vietnamese have become interested in art and ceramics. The prices of antiquities have increased, especially Trinh and imperial bleu de Hue. Dealers have begun to import Vietnamese ceramics and Chinese porcelains from Thailand and Europe back into Vietnam. In 1999, Vietnamese collectors and scholars, generally those working for museums and universities, were regrouped as the Vietnamese government reorganized their institutions. This happened first in Thang Long (Hanoi, 1999), then Thien Truong (Nam Dinh, 2004), Thanh Hoa (2004), Kinh Bac (Bac Ninh, 2009), Hai Phong (2009), and finally Ho Chi Minh City (2009). Their members are officially recognized by the government, can obtain assistance for their activities from the Ministry of Culture, be invited by the museums to participate in exhibitions, and exchange information and objects. These associations can organize exhibitions and sale auctions themselves. Vietnamese ceramics have found wide interest inside the country, as shown by extensive studies, books, and exhibitions.

Exhibitions have been organized throughout the world—in Belgium, Austria, United States, Germany, France, Switzerland, Singapore—though the interest of international museums has not escalated as fast as it appeared it might around the time of the Hoi An auctions, hindered by the forgery problems mentioned above. Vietnamese ceramics still remain of greatest interest within Vietnam. However, this is a passionate domain with its own characteristics and temptations, a world awaiting discovery, with new findings constantly arising, inspiring debate over questions of dating and production in the minds of art-lovers and scholars.

CAT. 34

CAT. 117

CAT. 19

CAT. 120

CAT. 128

# DECORATIVE MOTIFS ON VIETNAMESE CERAMICS

DONALD A. WOOD

The Vietnamese are profoundly aware of the world that surrounds them. Colorful flowers, dense forests, lush rice paddies, rushing streams and rivers, all play an important role in their life. Likewise, the animals, birds, and fish that inhabit this world are part of the everyday vocabulary in the lives of the Vietnamese. This variety of flora and fauna translates well into the art forms that developed over time in Vietnam, the most ubiquitous of which is perhaps ceramics. The decoration of bowls, plates, cups, jars, figurines and containers of all kinds offer a glimpse into what was important, significant, or amusing to the Vietnamese through the ages.

Vietnam is a close neighbor of China, and was ruled by China for a thousand years, during which time it was directly exposed to Chinese civilization and its ceramic industry. Yet Vietnamese potters did not simply copy Chinese ceramics and their decorative themes. Instead, they combined indigenous and Chinese elements in original ways, experimenting with new ideas and adopting features from other cultures as well, such as Cambodia, India, and Champa. Using native motifs, materials, and genius, the Vietnamese created some of the most beautiful and sophisticated ceramics in Southeast Asia.

Sometimes the decoration of the ceramics is simply that: decorative. However, often the decoration has further intrinsic meaning that explains the use or the importance of the piece. Everyday wares as opposed to ceremonial pieces are often identified by their

CAT. 116

decoration, and auspicious symbols together with mundane elements from everyday life are all depicted in Vietnamese ceramics. Geometric motifs and floral designs, animals (both mythological and real), scenes of people, clouds and religious symbols may all be found painted on Vietnamese ceramics. Incised, carved and appliquéd decorations were also done by the Vietnamese potters.

Decorations on Vietnamese ceramics in the collection of the Birmingham Museum of Art fall under the following headings:

| | |
|---|---|
| Plants | Landscapes |
| Animal, mythical and real | Buddhist Symbols |
| Water Creatures | Zodiac Signs |
| Birds | Chinese Characters |
| People | Decorative Motifs |

## PLANTS

### Lotus

The Lotus is a perennial plant thought to have originated in India that now grows all over Asia. Found wherever there is still, muddy water, the flowers of the plant are greatly admired for their color and shape. White, red, or pink, they sometimes tower above the water and the huge round leaves that surround them. Because the flowers push through the dark, murky waters to bloom in the clean sunlight above, Buddhists liken the lotus to the human spirit, which can rise above the problems of our mundane world to reach the pure state of enlightenment. The lotus is one of the Eight Treasures (Eight Auspicious Symbols) within Buddhist iconography:

- Conch – Buddha's thoughts
- Lotus – purity and enlightenment
- Wheel of the Law – knowledge
- Parasol – protection
- Mystic Knot – harmony
- Pair of Golden Fish – conjugal happiness and freedom
- Victory Banner – victorious battle
- Treasure Vase – endless wealth

The lotus represents the seventh month of the lunar calendar. The entire lotus plant is edible and is harvested in late summer when the seeds have matured. The seeds are roasted or candied and eaten as a snack, while the leaves are used as a flavoring and as wrappers in which to steam rice and other foods. The roots are harvested and cooked in a variety of ways, most commonly in stir-fry or soups; they can also be eaten raw.

Parts of the lotus are used for their medicinal value in Asia, particularly the seeds. They are sweet and neutral in taste and so are thought to benefit the spleen, kidney, and heart. The leaves of the plant are also considered neutral and benefit the spleen, stomach, and liver.

Within the Birmingham collection, the lotus appears as decoration, alone or in combination with other auspicious designs, and as carved accents on a variety of pieces. From everyday bowls and bottles (cat. 29 &158) to ceremonial and presentation pieces (cat. 11, 12, 17, 64, 116 & 124), the lotus is one of the most commonly found and beloved decorations on Vietnamese pottery.

## Chrysanthemum

The Chrysanthemum has been cultivated in China and discussed in its literature since at least the fifteenth century BCE. From there it spread to the rest of Asia where, adapting to Chinese symbolism, it represents the tenth month of the lunar calendar and the desire for long life.

The flower petals of the chrysanthemum do not fall like those of other flowers such as the rose. They are therefore an ideal offering to be placed on an altar as they hold their shape and retain their color for quite some time.

The chrysanthemum was also widely used as a medicine. The boiled roots were used as a headache remedy and the leaves were brewed and ingested as an aid for the liver and eyesight, and for reducing high blood pressure. The flowers and leaves were enjoyed as food in a number of dishes in Vietnam.

The chrysanthemums that appear on Vietnamese ceramics are not the large pompom flowers that are so proudly displayed at homes and gardens in the fall. Instead they are a medium bloom, often with only a single row of petals that form the central portion of a floral and vine design painted on to the clay. There appears to be no preferred number of petals for the flower as in some countries, for example, in Japan, where sixteen petals designate an Imperial chrysanthemum. Instead there can be as few as six or seven petals when the flower is shown in profile, or over thirty when the petals are sculpted to form the outside of a bowl or plate.

The chrysanthemum seems to have been a particularly favorite motif of the potters who worked with underglaze-blue decoration. Bowls, jars, and dishes of every shape and size with chrysanthemum floral designs show the popularity of this pattern. (cat. 115, 117 & 143)

## Peony

The peony is a favorite decorative motif in Asia. Found on paintings, textiles, lacquerware, and ceramics in Southeast Asia, China, and Japan, it is considered a flower of good fortune that symbolizes wealth and honor. In full bloom the peony is also a token of love, affection, and voluptuous female beauty. In addition, it is considered the principal flower of spring, the third month in the lunar calendar.

The peony has long been used for medicinal purposes. While all parts of the plant are considered beneficial, the roots and bark of the stem are thought to be particularly efficacious. Infused, they are believed to nourish the blood and to relieve pain.

The lush full blooms of the peony are often found as the central decoration in Vietnamese blue-and-white ceramics, and carved and molded designs as well. They are usually surrounded by scrolling leaf patterns and are found on plates, jars, flasks, cups, etc. The peony is the primary decoration on perhaps the most famous piece of Vietnamese blue-and-white, the large bottle at the Topkapi Saray Museum, Istanbul, dated to 1450. (cat. 43, 53, 123 & 131)

## Vines and Leaves

Vines and leaves are everywhere in Vietnam. Given the tropical climate of the area, they grow profusely and quickly. As such, the twirling, scrolling vine patterns and infinite variety of leaves are a ubiquitous design within Vietnamese ceramics. It is difficult to determine sometimes exactly what plant is intended. Lotus, chrysanthemum, and peony leaves can be fairly easily identified, but the curlicue, twisting lines of other climbers, while perhaps rooted in reality, can also be fanciful interpretations of the indigenous vegetation. Carved, molded, painted, and applied, vines and leaves are one of the most common of decorations within the ceramic decorations of Vietnam. (cat. 19, 44, 77 & 124)

CAT. 24

CAT. 166

CAT. 121

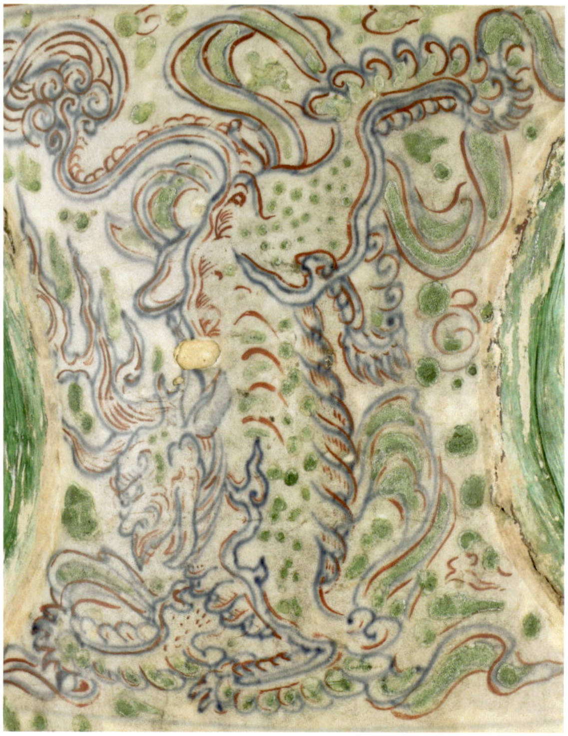

## ANIMALS: MYTHICAL AND REAL

### Dragon

According to ancient myth, the Vietnamese consider themselves descendants of a dragon and a fairy. As such, the dragon is among the preeminent Vietnamese mythological and cosmological beasts. Visible and invisible, the size of a silk worm or as big as the heavens, it is a benign creature that portends good luck and auspicious events. For the Vietnamese the dragon is essential, as it brings the rain that heralds the beginning of the growing season. It can change the weather at will and is responsible for the growth of the crops.

The Vietnamese dragon has many similarities in overall appearance to that of its Chinese neighbor. The body is slender and flowing with the head of a lion, a large nose and horns, canine teeth, curving whiskers, and pronounced scales. The thin feet usually have four or five claws. As in China, the Vietnamese dragon is found often amongst clouds and whirling mists where he sometimes chases and protects the flaming pearl of wisdom. However, it is also shown with flowers, a combination not common in Chinese iconography (cat. 27).

The potters of Vietnam loved the dragon. The creature appears on vessels of all shapes and sizes and in virtually every decorative technique. The potters show an especially playful sense with the use of dragons for handles and spouts. On some vessels the dragon plunges into the upper shoulder of one side of an ewer, the end of its body forming the handle, while the front of the creature claws its way through the clay on the other side where its head forms the spout. (cat. 10, 24, 80 & 166)

### Kylan, or Qilin

The Kylan is a popular animal motif on underglaze-blue and overglaze enamel-decorated Vietnamese ceramics (cat. 121). The creature is a mythical beast of Chinese origin, known all over Asia, and is an auspicious symbol and portent of good fortune. The Kylan has a benign personality and is so gentle that it can walk among grass and flowers without damaging them.

The appearance of the Kylan is a composite animal. It has hoofed feet like an ox, a dragon-like head, deer antlers, the skin and scales of a fish, and the tail of a lion. Its head is often shown surrounded by flame-like vapors. In the past Westerners have called the Kylan a unicorn, while among Chinese of the Ming dynasty (1368–1644) it was equated with the giraffe.

### Taotie

The Taotie is a popular animal design in early Chinese art. It appears on bronzes, ceramics, jades, bone, and other stone carvings. The creature is a composite animal, facing front, symmetrical with eyes, nose, ears, and horns. Thought to have religious or ceremonial meaning, it is not clear what this powerful animal symbolized to the ancient Chinese.

In Vietnamese artifacts the Taotie survives on early bronze and ceramic forms. The ceramics in particular are found in burial contexts and appear to be replicas of bronzes with ring handles suspended from the masks. The stylized masks as handles on the Chinese inspired Hu-shaped jar from the first to the third century are a classic example (cat. 7).

### Magic/Winged Horse

The horse figures in many Vietnamese tales. For example, King Ly Cong Uan (974–1028), founder of the Ly dynasty (1009–1225), is said to have had a vision of a white horse that showed him where to build his capital, Hanoi. As a result the white horse is the patron animal of the city and is honored with a temple called the *Bach Ma,* or White Horse, temple. This is not unlike the vision of a white horse that prompted the construction of the first Buddhist temple *(Baima Si)* in Louyang, China in 68 CE under the patronage of Emperor Ming of the Eastern Han dynasty (25–220). The horse is the seventh of the Chinese zodiac animals.

The horse has many Buddhist associations as well. Kantaka was the favorite horse of Siddhartha Gautama and carried his master during the ceremonial departure from his palace. Seven horses draw the chariot of Surya, the Sun god. The winged horse is often shown in Buddhist art carrying a sacred book on its back or simply in conjunction with other sacred animals such as those on the Birmingham jar (cat. 121). The wings are of note in that they are not the feathered wings of Pegasus, but appear instead to be a membrane, like a bat's wing.

### Other Mythical Animals

There are numerous other, unidentifiable mythical animals shown on Vietnamese ceramics. Most are hoofed quadrupeds in galloping poses shown among clouds or *ru-yi* patterns. They resemble lions and horses of various kinds, but with individual features that set them apart and show a vivid imagination for the real and unreal (cat. 128).

### Lion

The lion is not native to Vietnam but was once common in parts of Central Asia, ancient Persia, and India, and is an early symbol of power and authority in Hinduism and Buddhism. In Hindu iconography the lion appears as the vehicle for the goddesses Durga and Parvati. In Buddhism, Shakyamuni is called the Lion of the Shakya clan, and lions are often shown to either side of his throne. It was through Hinduism and Buddhism that the symbol of the lion was introduced throughout Asia.

In Vietnam the lion appears in Chinese and Buddhist contexts, primarily in pairs as the guardians of buildings and as the centerpiece in the traditional Lion Dance at New Year. Thought to have originated in India, the Lion Dance is part of festivals and celebrations throughout Asia.

In Vietnamese ceramics lions appear in the central panels of underglaze blue-and-white and polychrome decorated plates. Like other beasts in Vietnamese wares, whirling clouds or *ru-yi* patterns often surround the animal. The lion is also occasionally found in sculpted ceramic forms. A vessel in the shape of a caparisoned lion, covered in a cream-colored glaze, was perhaps used as a water dropper, to add water to an ink stone when grinding ink for writing or painting (cat. 32).

### Tiger

The tiger is the mythological guardian of the West and a symbol of autumn in ancient Chinese cosmology. Tigers were believed to live hundreds of years, turning white as they aged. They form an integral part of Vietnamese lore and legends, such as *A Tiger, a Worm, and a Snail, The Shrine to the Last Tiger of Vung Tau,* etc.

Tigers were, and still are, an important part of traditional Asian medicine, including Vietnam. This is especially true in China where the continuing demand for tiger parts has decimated the populations of the animal in China and Southeast Asia. The parts of the tiger most prized for medicinal purposes are the penis, believed to improve virility, and the eyes, that help clarify vision.

Tigers appear infrequently as a decorative motif in Vietnamese ceramics; there is only one example in the Birmingham collection, a jar from Champa (cat. 164) that has four feline lug handles. Each cat has on its forehead the Chinese character *wang* (meaning king) formed by the horizontal black stripes of their fur. Thus nature identified them as "king of the jungle."

### Deer

The deer is another animal found primarily as decoration on the central panels of plates painted in underglaze-blue and polychrome enamels. Gamboling among clouds, by a river or through a landscape, the deer appear to be both mythical and real.

The deer is thought to live a very long time and is the only animal that can search out and find the fungus of immortality. Deer horn is a much sought-after traditional medicine throughout Asia. It is believed effective for the treatment of arthritis, as an anti-aging agent, and the promotion of good health in general (cat. 118).

### Dog

The dog is part of ancient Vietnamese mythology. In one story a dog helps a king defeat an enemy and so wins the hand of his daughter the princess. They marry and have children who then found various tribes within Vietnam. As a result, the dog is greatly respected in many parts of Vietnam.

The dog is not a particularly common decoration in Vietnamese ceramics. Some depictions of dogs in Vietnam may actually be foxes. Legends of nine-tailed foxes are popular in China and may have influenced the multiple tails seen on some images of Vietnamese dogs, or foxes (cat. 69). In these tales transformation and possession are the primary attributes of the fox, but some are also love stories where a fox becomes a beautiful young lady who falls in love with a man.

The dog in Asia is valued for its fidelity as a loyal companion and protector, and an approaching dog is a sign of impending good fortune. Yet the dog is also looked down upon as a scavenger.. The dog is the eleventh animal in the Chinese zodiac.

## WATER CREATURES

### Fish

Fish are a staple of the Vietnamese diet. From pond, canal, river, and ocean, fresh, dried, or made into a sauce,

CAT. 118

CAT. 119

fish are consumed in large quantities on a daily basis. Fishing and farming were the primary occupations of traditional Vietnam. Fishing, in particular, went on year round with no seasonal restrictions to hinder the catch. Fish and fishing abound in Vietnamese tales and mythology. They are part of nearly every celebration, especially New Year's and weddings, where gifts of fish form a wish for abundance, many offspring, and marital bliss.

The fish is also one of the Eight Treasures of Buddhism symbolizing freedom from all restraints. As the fish moves easily in any direction within its element, water, it is a metaphor for the fully emancipated spirit that knows no bounds or restrictions.

Fish are one of the most common decorations on Vietnamese ceramics. Painted, carved, molded, stamped, or applied, they are found on plates, bowls, jars, and cups of all shapes and sizes. Many different types of fish are shown within Vietnamese iconography. Carp, catfish, and needlefish, among others, are often depicted in extremely realistic detail. They can also be drawn quickly in an almost cartoon manner, showing the skill and dexterity of the anonymous artisan. Alone, in pairs, in schools, or simply hinted at by tails flapping in waves, the fish swim amidst waterweeds or float languidly in calm pools (cat. 36, 119 & 126).

## Frogs and Toads

Frogs and toads appear as decoration on Southeast Asian bronze drums from as early as 1500 BCE. The frogs and toads are believed to represent rain and may have played a vital role in ceremonies that brought, and perhaps stopped, the monsoon rains. The drums are often found in burial contexts. The frog and toad are also favorite characters in many Vietnamese folk tales and fables, with the frog sometimes replacing the dragon in the creation myth of the Vietnamese people. Frogs and toads are believed to live very long lives.

Frogs are part of the Vietnamese diet and are also used in traditional medicine. Dried and reconstituted, various parts of the frog are thought to be good for the complexion, lungs, and kidneys, for respiratory problems, coughing and night sweats.

In ceramics the frog or toad is often found very realistically portrayed as sculpted pieces that are used as water droppers. Careful attention is paid to their size, the warts and patterns on the skin, as well as the alert stare of the creature as it is perhaps about to pounce on its prey. Green and olive green glazes add to the natural appearance of the creatures (cat. 50).

## Tortoise and Turtles

The tortoise is believed to live ten thousand years. It is the symbol of longevity and endurance, and represents the double symbol of heaven and earth, the domed part of its shell being heaven, the flat underside being the earth. It presides over the north in traditional Chinese cosmology.

The Vietnamese eat tortoises and turtles. Their dried shells are powdered to form a traditional medicine that is thought to be good for arthritis and diseases of the kidneys. Tortoises and turtles can often be bought outside Buddhist temples where it is considered meritorious to purchase and then free them in the pools around the temple compound.

The incised pattern of the shell of the tortoise and turtle is a popular design on the inside of Vietnamese bowls. Likewise, the spotted yellow and brown color of tortoiseshell decorates the outside of some bowls. These can be very similar to the patterns used on Chinese tea bowls. The turtle is also found carved in low relief on the inside of some bowls and as a free-standing figure used for water droppers decorated in underglaze blue (cat. 71, 72, 95 & 136).

### Waves

While waves and water are found as part of the decoration with many of the water creatures, they are also used as the primary decoration on some pieces. Rows and rows of carved waves with fishtails appearing above them decorate the insides of two bowls in the Birmingham collection (cat. 36 & 37). This design can also be found in Chinese Yaozhou ware bowls of the Northern Song dynasty (960–1127).

CAT. 121

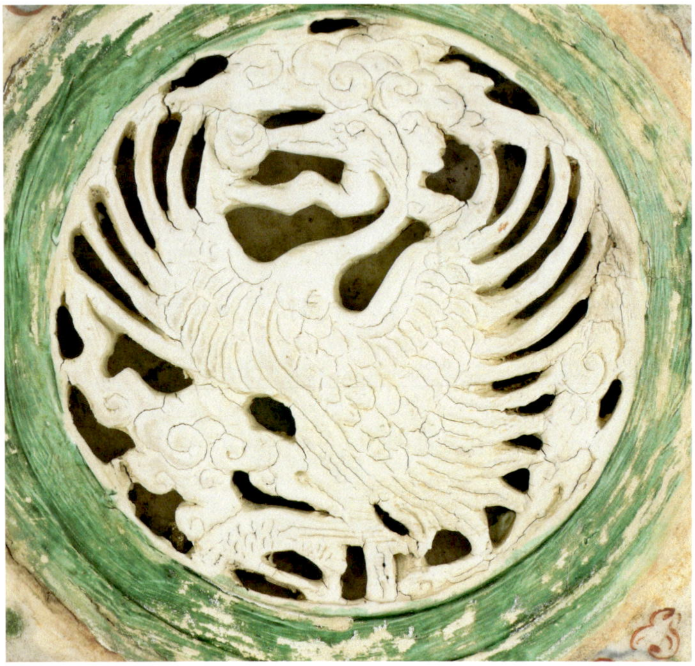

## BIRDS

### Crane

The Crane and the Dragon are two of the most auspicious creatures of Vietnam. The crane in particular, with its great size, loud trumpeting calls and spectacular mating dance is a traditional symbol of long life and immortality throughout Vietnam. Numerous tales and legends about the crane abound and it is often shown in conjunction with a tortoise or deer, a pine tree or rock, or carrying Immortals on its back as they fly together through the heavens. There are said to be four kinds of cranes, white, black, yellow, and blue, with the black reaching the remarkable age of six hundred years.

The crane was also one of the animals designating different court rank within the Chinese-based administrative system. Within the Civilian rankings it was the first, or highest of bureaucratic appointments.

As common as the crane is within Vietnamese legend and tales, it is not found frequently as a motif on ceramics within the Birmingham collection. One example is a lidded bowl in which two cranes are deftly carved on the inside of the bowl flying around a central lotus bud (cat. 56). Another is a large polychrome jar with four cranes carved in reticulated round bisque-fired panels that are inset into the walls of the jar and then backed with plain clay, creating a sense of depth to the composition. The crane panels are intricately carved, the birds poised with outstretched wings amidst curling clouds (cat. 121).

### Red Bird

The Red, or Vermilion, Bird is often equated with Vietnam. The iconography dates back to Chinese antiquity where the Red Bird is the creature that represents the south and is associated with summer and fire. The Red Bird was considered a divine messenger and harbinger of good things to come. Numerous red or reddish-brown birds are found in Vietnam, but no real bird is particularly associated with the mythical bird. It is depicted with features that can be a combination of birds, such as the peacock, partridge, and pheasant among others.

CAT. 125

Like the crane, the Red Bird is an auspicious symbol. Birds on an elaborate seventeenth-century incense-burner in the Birmingham collection may represent the auspicious Red Bird (cat. 165). The incense-burner is covered with carved and appliquéd decorations, including dragons and two birds. Spots on the opposite side of the incense burner may have been decorated with similar appliquéd birds. Individually made and applied, the birds have crests upon their heads, large wings, and prominent tail-feathers.

### Parrot

The parrot is a much-loved bird in Vietnam, not only for its colorful display of feathers but also for its ability to mimic human speech. They represent the South, distinct from China in the North. Various types of parrots are native to Vietnam and they are often kept as pets. At times they have also been considered a delicacy within Vietnamese cuisine.

The parrot is often found as a decoration on Vietnamese ceramics. Ewers, cups, and brush-washers are shaped like the bird and decorated in both underglaze-blue and overglaze polychrome enamel wares (cat. 129 & 130), with highlights realistically carved and picked out in colors. The parrot is also found decorating reticulated carved panels that are bisque-fired and inset into ewers, as well as painted in the center of large plates.

### Duck

The duck is considered a symbol of happiness throughout Vietnam. The Mandarin Duck in particular is thought to mate for life and one will pine away if separated from the other. The duck is a popular subject in embroidery and wedding-related materials.

A common food, duck is considered a "cool" food within the *yin* and *yang* of Vietnamese cooking and so is served in the summer, or the "hot" season. Dried duck-body parts, such as the gizzard, are also used in traditional Vietnamese medicines.

Ducks decorate a variety of Vietnamese ceramics. They are quickly sketched in underglaze-blue or in polychrome enamels on jars, bottles, plates, and covered boxes. Perhaps the most charming representations are pairs of Mandarin Ducks swimming together, shaped as water-droppers (cat. 137). Features and feathers are carefully picked out in underglaze-blue as the two ducks nestle together.

## PEOPLE

With all the careful observation of the world around them, it is interesting that depictions of people are not common in Vietnamese ceramics. In early pieces, faces, or masks, of figures are found on roof tile ends and what appears to be a stamp (cat. 2, 3, 8 & 9). In later wares there are occasional formal vessels shaped like kneeling attendants or officials, but few pieces decorated with what one would consider scenes of people.

A *kendi* in the Birmingham collection that shows groups of standing figures among pine trees and grasses is one of two such very unusual examples in the Birmingham collection. Dressed in large hats and

CAT. 3

CAT. 35

skirts, the figures are perhaps meant to represent foreigners. The whole is skillfully painted in underglaze cobalt blue (cat. 125).

Another example is a small brown bowl with three molded figures set between Buddhist symbols in the cavetto of the bowl. One of the figures is dressed in a tunic while the others wear longer robes. Patterns in the clothes are simply rendered and resemble more indigenous textiles and styles than the figures on the *kendi* (84). Two modified Chinese characters in the center of the bowl read *guanyao* ("official ware").

More common are images of baby boys playing amidst flowers and scrolling vines in Vietnamese ceramics. Based on Chinese wares of the Song and Jin dynasties (960–1279, 1115–1234), the motif represents the desire for many sons (cat. 51, 53 & 54).

While landscapes decorate many Vietnamese wares, landscapes with figures are unusual. An example in the Birmingham collection is a large plate with underglaze-blue and polychrome decoration (cat. 120) dating to the sixteenth century. Two figures in long robes stand in the foreground amidst flowering plants and trees that recede into a mountain landscape. The scene is quickly but skillfully painted and is reminiscent of Chinese landscapes found on ceramics from southern China at the same time.

## BUDDHIST MOTIFS

Buddhism came to Vietnam perhaps as early as the second century from China to the north and via the sea routes from India in the south. The religion enjoyed a cooperative and harmonious existence in Vietnam with both Chinese Daoist and indigenous beliefs.

Buddhist motifs appear on many Vietnamese ceramics of all shapes and sizes. Among the more elaborate of these designs are the Eight Treasures of Buddhism described in the section on the Lotus Flower. Found as a complete group (cat. 123), or select portions of the group (cat. 70 & 108), these Treasures are most commonly painted in underglaze blue, but are also used as carved decorative motifs.

The Flaming Pearl is also represented on ritual vessels (cat. 125). Believed to grant all wishes and to be a symbol of wisdom, the pearl appears alone or with other Buddhist symbols such as the double *vajra* (cat. 122). The *vajra* is a symbol of hardness and is indestructible like a diamond. It is equated with the eternal powers of the Buddha's teachings.

Buddhist figures and immortals are found appliquéd on some vessels, particularly on some later wares from Bát Tràng (cat. 167).

The swastika is also found painted on Vietnamese ceramics. This is an ancient auspicious symbol in India that is commonly found in Hindu and Buddhist art. The Eight Trigrams of Chinese origin are also used as decoration on this bowl. The Trigrams have been part of divination practices, in conjunction with the classic Yi Jing, since ancient times in China. This combination of Buddhist (tortoise and swastikas) and Daoist (trigrams) decoration is a good indication of the synchretic mixture of religious beliefs traditionally prevalent in Vietnam (cat. 71).

## CHINESE CHARACTERS

Chinese characters were traditionally employed to write classical Chinese and the Sino-Vietnamese vocabulary in Vietnam. The characters were used for their original meanings in writing loan words from Chinese and, as with Japanese *kanji* and Korean *hanja,* were adapted and adopted to write the native Vietnamese. Given the strong Chinese influences in Vietnamese culture, it comes as no surprise that Chinese characters are found on some Vietnamese ceramics. For example, the inscription on the large jar with the appliquéd Buddhist figures not only forms a poem, but the calligraphy itself is beautifully written and spaced so that it becomes an integral part of the overall decorative scheme (cat. 167).

Two characters appear on the bottom of an early steamer (*Ping San,* cat. 4). This could be the name of the potter who made the piece. If so, he was probably Chinese, as the Vietnamese at this time most likely did not have knowledge of written Chinese. However, a signed piece of pottery at such an early time would be very unusual. (See *Vietnamese Ceramics: A Separate Tradition,* pages 29 and 179, for further discussion of this piece.)

Single characters are also found on a variety of wares. A small dish has the Chinese character *dai* (great) carved as the central decoration (cat. 73), while a variety of small bowls and cups with the character *fu* (good fortune, *phuc* in Vietnamese) written in underglaze-blue in the center are common. There are numerical inscriptions as well on some pieces that were perhaps intended as identification numbers of some sort, such as the characters for 'ninety' carved into the bottom of an incense burner (cat. 35).

## DESIGNS AND PATTERNS

There are numerous other designs and patterns that help create the overall appearance of a piece of Vietnamese ceramic. Clouds, lappets, stripes, and lines, and chatter marks all serve this purpose.

Clouds are an auspicious sign symbolizing happiness and good fortune. They are found in early Chinese art from the Han dynasty (206 BCE–220 CE) as wisps of vapor speeding across the heavens with the Immortals on stone, lacquer, and ceramic artifacts. In Vietnam, a country that weathers typhoons and frequent rain, the changing clouds are a daily reminder of the blessings and destructive capabilities of nature.

The earliest depictions of clouds on Vietnamese ceramics in the Birmingham collection are appliquéd examples that appear on the shoulders of several twelfth- to thirteenth-century ewers (cat. 23 & 24). The clouds are the primary decoration of these pieces and so assume a position of importance not found in other examples. Small carved and appliquéd clouds are also found on a much later seventeenth-century Incense Burner (cat. 165) as part of a register of decoration surrounding what appears to be the sun. In underglaze cobalt blue, clouds are part of the decoration on several later examples in the collection. A large fifteenth- to sixteenth-century charger has a mythical beast cavorting amid a dense surrounding cloud pattern, while a large eighteenth-century jar sports dragons chasing flaming pearls as they race through clouds on the shoulder of the jar (cat. 128 & 166).

Lappets or petals form the primary carved decoration on some Vietnamese ceramics (cat. 216 & 217) and are painted in underglaze cobalt blue to outline other motifs such as flaming pearls and vegetation (cat. 132). Lappets are often found painted in underglaze cobalt blue in rows on the underside of the rims of many pieces.

Raised carved lines are used for their decorative effect. Often lines are used simply to demarcate and accentuate the divisions within a piece, such as the foot, body, and shoulder (cat. 62, 75 & 91).

Likewise chatter marks serve as a quick, simple way to add surface design and pattern to a variety of bowls and dishes (cat. 89 & 208).

In summary, the Vietnamese show an endless creativity in the decoration of their rich and varied ceramic tradition. Nature, man, and pure design all played a part in their imagery. Much of the iconography has meaning or symbolic significance, while other works are simply decorative and playful. The Vietnamese ceramic tradition owes much to foreign influence, but also shows a strong indigenous desire to work with what is important and found daily in the lives of the Vietnamese.

CAT. 1 – 9

# HAN–VIET

From the first to the fourth centuries CE, northern Vietnam was occupied and administered by China. Ceramics were made in Chinese shapes using the light-colored clays of the Red River Valley. Often these "Han–Viet" ceramics bear deliberate splashes of green glaze (sometimes regularly spaced, they are not accidental kiln drips); this may have been a hint that the potters knew about the green lead glaze common on the ceramics of Han China or perhaps they were meant to echo the color of bronze. The incense-burner here (6) bears an unusually large, and beautiful, expanse of green glaze.

Chinese forms included oval "ear-cups" (1), a shape made from several different materials in China (such as wood and lacquer), also a number of formal shapes that in China were made of bronze. An example of a Vietnamese piece that follows a Chinese bronze model is the well-potted *hu* displayed here (7), with its tall elegant silhouette and two stylized *taotie* masks applied to the shoulder.

The underside of the cover of the steamer (4) bears two Chinese characters (perhaps a name?), suggesting that the person who made this piece may have been expatriate Chinese, as it is unlikely that a Vietnamese potter at this time would have been literate in Chinese. Clay models of houses and farms often accompanied the body in Han Chinese tombs. Equivalents have been found in Vietnam, though the roof of the model house here (5) represents thatch and reeds—a reflection of Vietnam's riverine culture—rather than the tiled roofs of Chinese models.

Semicircular Vietnamese roof-tiles dating to the Han–Viet period (2, 3), and to following centuries (8), often ended in flat circles depicting grimacing faces, probably to scare away evil spirits. Maybe the little stamp with grinning face (9) was a child's toy.

CAT. 1

## EAR-CUP

Han-Viet period, 1st–4th century
Stoneware with green and buff ash glaze
1 ½ x 5 ¼ inches
Collection of the Art Fund, Inc. at the Birmingham Museum of Art; Bequest of William M. Spencer III AFI139.2010

CAT. 2

## TILE-END

Han-Viet period, 1st–4th century
Stoneware with demon mask
5 1/4 x 5 1/4 inches
Collection of the Art Fund, Inc. at the
Birmingham Museum of Art; Bequest of
William M. Spencer III AFI140.2010

CAT. 3

## TILE-END

Han-Viet period, 1st–4th century
Stoneware with demon mask
1/2 x 3 3/4 inches
Collection of the Art Fund, Inc. at the
Birmingham Museum of Art; Bequest of
William M. Spencer III AFI141.2010

INSCRIPTION

CAT. 4

## STEAMER

Han-Viet period, 1st–4th century
Inscribed: Ping-san (?)
Stoneware with green and buff ash glaze
with twisted-rope decoration
4 1/4 x 6 inches
Collection of the Art Fund, Inc. at the
Birmingham Museum of Art; Bequest of
William M. Spencer III AFI62.2010a-b

CAT. 5

## MODEL HOUSE

Han-Viet period, 1st–4th century
Stoneware model house with reed roof
and cut-out walls
7 ¾ x 8 x 8 ¼ inches
Collection of the Art Fund, Inc. at the
Birmingham Museum of Art; Bequest of
William M. Spencer III AFI120.2010a-b

CAT. 6

## INCENSE BURNER

Han-Viet period, 1st–4th century
Glazed stoneware with incised line decoration
7 ⅜ x 8 ¾ inches
Collection of the Art Fund, Inc. at the Birmingham
Museum of Art; Bequest of William M. Spencer III
AFI138.2010a-b

**CAT. 7**

## JAR (HU)

Han-Viet period, 1st–4th century
Glazed stoneware with buff ash glaze and green splash, applied taotie masks
11 ¼ x 7 ½ inches
Museum purchase with funds provided by Helen Hudgens 2009.6

CAT. 8

## TILE-END

Annam period, 7th–8th century
Reportedly from Quang Nam
Stoneware with Gorgon or demon mask
2 ¾ x 6 15⁄16 inches
Collection of the Art Fund, Inc. at the Birmingham Museum of Art; Bequest of William M. Spencer III
AFI142.2010

CAT. 9

## STAMP

Annam period, 7th–8th century
Stoneware with grinning face
1 5⁄8 x 1 5⁄8 inches
Collection of the Art Fund, Inc. at the Birmingham Museum of Art; Bequest of William M. Spencer III AFI143.2010

**CAT. 10–22**

# LY DYNASTY
## (1009–1225)

In 1009, the leader of the Ly clan gained control of northern Vietnam with the assistance of the Buddhist establishment, and settled his capital at Thang Long, meaning "Rising Dragon," on the site of modern Hanoi. Under this first native dynasty, Vietnamese culture blossomed. Indigenous Vietnamese forms were explored and distinctly Vietnamese decorative themes were developed; dragons and lotus flowers were especially popular motifs. The dragon that decorates a hollow brick (10) is long and sinuous and differs from Chinese dragons. Found in Hanoi, this brick may have been part of the imperial palace in Thang Long. The creature in the medallion on the side of a beaker (16) is either a dragon or a mythical *kylan (qilin)*.

Lotuses are the archetypal symbols of Buddhism throughout East Asia. The lotus represents purity: it grows in water, its blossoms emerging unsullied from the mud. Individually carved lotus petals form the sides of small offering dishes (11, 12), and lotus-petal collars adorn the shoulders of large and small ewers (13, 14). Ewer (14) is a shape unique to Vietnam, its pedestal base reminding of twelfth-century baluster vases from the neighboring Khmer empire.

CAT. 10

## BRICK

Ly dynasty, 11th–13th century
Fired ceramic with pierced
and molded dragon decoration
5 1/2 x 6 7/8 x 5 3/4 inches
Collection of the Art Fund, Inc. at the
Birmingham Museum of Art; Bequest of
William M. Spencer III AFI134.2010

CAT. 11

## OFFERING PLATE

Ly dynasty, 11th–13th century
Glazed stoneware with incised lotus decoration and carved lotus-petal collar
1 1/4 x 5 1/8 inches
Collection of the Art Fund, Inc. at the Birmingham Museum of Art; Bequest of William M. Spencer III AFI83.2010

CAT. 12

## OFFERING PLATE

Ly dynasty, 11th–13th century
Glazed stoneware with incised lotus decoration and carved lotus-petal collar
¾ x 3 ⅛ inches
Collection of the Art Fund, Inc. at the Birmingham Museum of Art; Bequest of William M. Spencer III AFI144.2010

CAT. 13

## EWER

Ly dynasty, 11th–13th century
Glazed stoneware with carved lotus-petal collar
2 ¾ x 3 ¾ inches
Collection of the Art Fund, Inc. at the Birmingham Museum of Art; Bequest of William M. Spencer III
AFI115.2010

CAT. 14

## EWER

Ly dynasty, 11th–13th century
Glazed stoneware with animal spout,
carved lotus-petal collar, and pedestal base
6 3⁄4 x 7 inches
Collection of the Art Fund, Inc. at the Birmingham
Museum of Art; Bequest of William M. Spencer III
AFI124.2010

**CAT. 15**

## LAMP

Ly dynasty, 11th–14th century
Glazed stoneware
6 ⅜ x 4 ⅞ inches
Collection of the Art Fund, Inc. at the Birmingham
Museum of Art; Bequest of William M. Spencer III
AFI108.2010

## CAT. 16

# BEAKER

Ly dynasty, 11th–13th century
Glazed stoneware with row of bosses and
three molded dragon or kylan medallions,
faint chocolate wash to base
4 3/8 x 4 1/2 inches
Collection of the Art Fund, Inc. at the
Birmingham Museum of Art; Bequest of
William M. Spencer III AFI100.2010

CAT. 17–22

# BROWN-INLAID WARES

A popular form of decoration at the Cizhou kilns in Song China (960–1279) was to paint a design directly onto the surface of an unfired clay body (sometimes made lighter by applying a white slip), using an iron-brown pigment; the whole was then covered with a transparent glaze. Vietnam aimed for a similar visual result, but perhaps because they could not guarantee the transparency of their overglazes, Vietnamese potters developed a new technique to ensure that their designs remained visible. A wood-ash glaze that fired to a light ivory color was applied over the surface of the leather-hard clay, and a design was made by scraping away some of the still viscous glaze. The scraped areas were then inlaid with an iron-brown pigment, and the piece fired. The edges of the design were often deeply incised into the clay (19, 20).

This form of decoration technique was very popular in ceramics of the Ly (1009–1225) and Tran (1225–1400) dynasties, and is specific to Vietnam. The most common shape is a straight-sided or gently curving covered jar. These jars often have carved lotus-petal collars, the Buddhist connection with lotuses suggesting temple or burial use. The jars were most likely used to store food. Many have been excavated but it is rare to find two matching jars like 17 and 18; these examples have been companions for at least seven hundred years. The most common designs are scrolling vegetal patterns (19) and lotus blossoms (17, 18). Other inlaid-brown designs that have been found include indigenous long-tailed birds, sometimes elephants, and, very rarely, human figures.

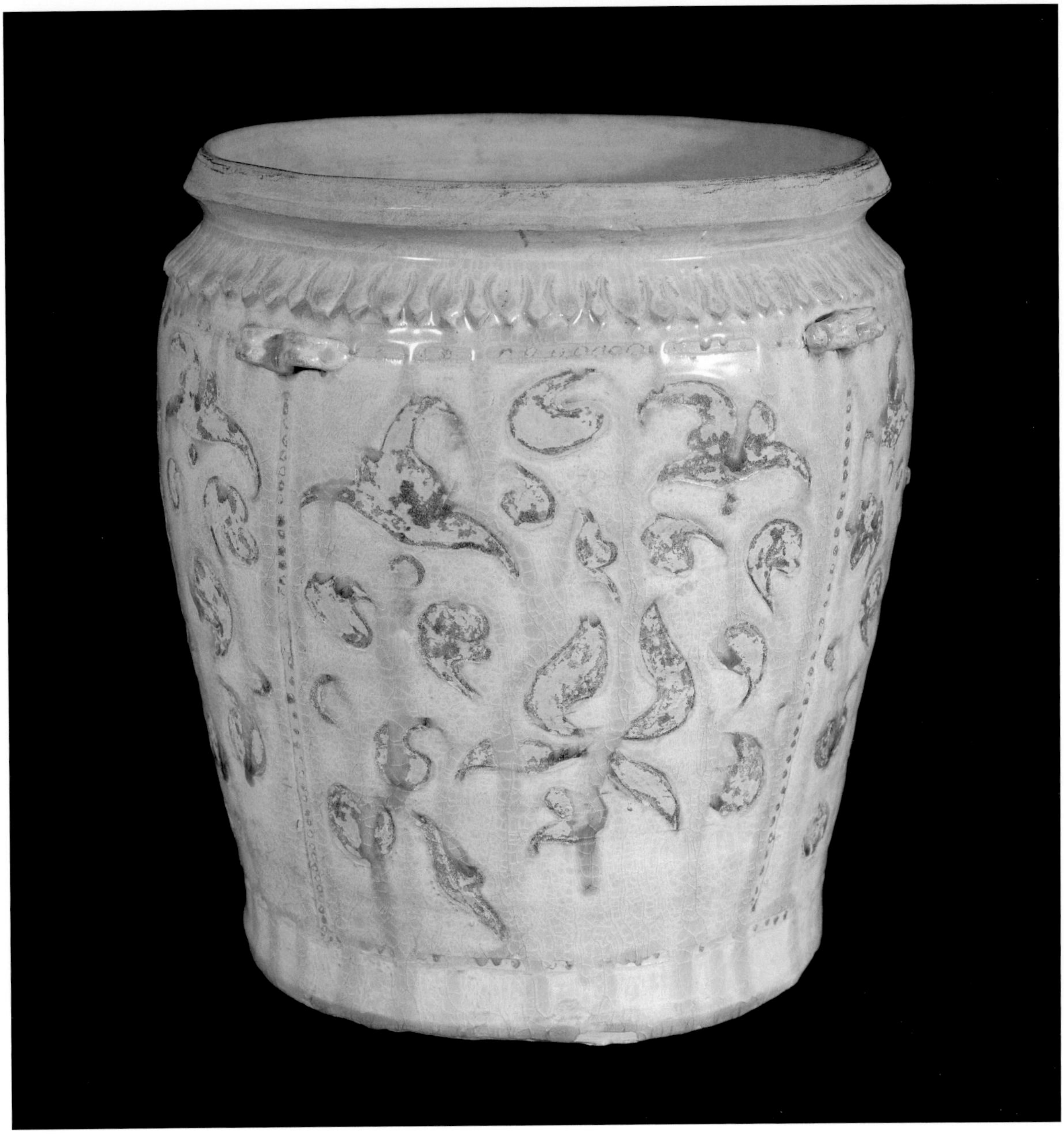

**CAT. 17**

## JAR

Ly–Tran dynasty, 12th–14th century
Glazed stoneware with carved lotus-petal collar,
four double-strap handles, and inlaid lotus decoration
12 x 11 3⁄8 inches
Collection of the Art Fund, Inc. at the Birmingham Museum of
Art; Bequest of William M. Spencer III AFI41.2010

**CAT.** 18

## JAR

Ly–Tran dynasty, 12th–14th century
Glazed stoneware with carved lotus-petal collar, four strap handles, inlaid lotus decoration
11 1/4 x 11 inches
Collection of the Art Fund, Inc. at the Birmingham Museum of Art; Bequest of William M. Spencer III
AFI145.2010

**CAT.** 19

## JAR

Ly–Tran dynasty, 12th–14th century
Glazed stoneware with carved lotus-petal collar, four strap handles and three bands of incised vegetal decoration
13 x 11 inches
Collection of the Art Fund, Inc. at the Birmingham Museum of Art; Bequest of William M. Spencer III AFI43.2010

CAT. 20

## JAR

Ly–Tran dynasty, 12th–14th century
Glazed stoneware
with inlaid vegetal decoration
6 3⁄8 x 7 3⁄4 inches
Collection of the Art Fund, Inc. at the Birmingham Museum of Art; Bequest of William M. Spencer III AFI39.2010

CAT. 21

## BASIN

Ly–Tran dynasty, 12th–14th century
Glazed stoneware
with inlaid vegetal decoration
4 1⁄8 x 8 3⁄8 inches
Collection of the Art Fund, Inc. at the Birmingham Museum of Art; Bequest of William M. Spencer III AFI54.2010

## CAT. 22

# BASIN

Ly–Tran dynasty, 12th–14th century
Glazed stoneware with inlaid vegetal decoration
6 ¼ x 11 ¼ inches
Collection of the Art Fund, Inc. at the Birmingham
Museum of Art; Bequest of William M. Spencer III
AFI146.2010

CAT. 23–26

# IVORY-GLAZED EWERS

A group of large, skillfully potted ivory-glazed ewers are unique to Birmingham's collection of Vietnamese ceramics. These ewers have full, round, bulbous bodies and are extremely thin-walled. Each has a spout in the form of a mythical animal: these include a *garuda* (birdlike creature, 25), a *makara* (aquatic monster with gills combining features of a crocodile and an elephant, 26), and two dragons. The handles of the two dragon-spouted ewers (23, 24) appear to lead the dragon's body through the vessel itself. The state of the glaze on these two ewers indicates that they spent centuries in water or waterlogged earth. Applied cloud motifs or rosettes adorn the shoulders of three of the four ewers. The covers of 23 and 25 are lobed like a lotus leaf. The handle shapes and the spiky details suggest that these ewers were based on metal prototypes. The flat-topped ewer (26) is a shape unique to Vietnam; matching holes were made in the lid and the walls of the ewer so that a piece of wood or bamboo could be passed through, securing the lid.

These fine ewers would probably have been used for wine or ritual use in the royal palace or a great Buddhist temple. They are extremely light; the beauty of their full and distinctive shapes and the skill of their manufacture place these ewers at the pinnacle of East Asian ceramic production.

**CAT. 23**

## EWER

Ly–Tran dynasty, 12th–14th century
Glazed stoneware with lobed lid, grooved knob with lotus-petal collar, dragon spout with handle in the shape of dragon's body, four applied cloud motifs with bands of low-relief petals around shoulder and above base
9 ½ x 11 ¾ inches
Collection of the Art Fund, Inc. at the Birmingham Museum of Art; Bequest of William M. Spencer III AFI40.2010a-b

**CAT. 24**

## EWER

Ly–Tran dynasty, 12th–14th century
Glazed stoneware with domed cover, lotus-petal collar, dragon spout with handle in the shape of dragon's body, four applied cloud motifs between raised lines
8 1/4 x 9 7/8 inches
Collection of the Art Fund, Inc. at the Birmingham Museum of Art; Bequest of William M. Spencer III AFI71.2010a-b

**CAT. 25**

## EWER

Ly–Tran dynasty, 12th–14th century
Glazed stoneware with lobed cover and grooved knob, garuda spout, spiral handle with carved bo leaf, and two applied rosettes
10 3/4 x 9 1/4 inches
Collection of the Art Fund, Inc. at the Birmingham Museum of Art; Bequest of William M. Spencer III AFI72.2010a-b

**CAT. 26**

## EWER

Ly–Tran dynasty, 11th–13th century
Glazed stoneware with flat-topped cover,
makara spout, stepped handle
7 x 7 inches
Collection of the Art Fund, Inc. at the
Birmingham Museum of Art; Bequest of
William M. Spencer III AFI51.2010a-b

CAT. 27–39

# IVORY-GLAZED WARES

The most popular glaze-type during the native Ly (1009–1225) and Tran (1225–1400) dynasties, a period when Vietnam consciously celebrated its independence from China, was an ivory color. The glaze was made from wood-ash containing about two percent iron; when the iron content reached about four percent, the ash glaze fired to a green color; and six percent iron gave a rich chocolate brown. Here again we see decorative dragon motifs (27, 28) and lotus petals (30, 38). Lotus petals are carved on the exterior of a large bowl (29), with a lotus spray on the interior.

An ivory-gray incense-burner (35) has Chinese characters meaning "ninety" incised into its base, perhaps a potter's mark or a batch number. A beaker (38) has a smooth white glaze and a carved exterior representing lotus petals. This beaker and a fluted bowl (39) are unusually finely potted and thin-walled, though the kiln grit in the cavetto of the fluted bowl and the tendency of its glaze to lift are deficiencies that the Chinese would have rejected.

This grouping demonstrates several distinctly Vietnamese shapes. These include the sharply inverted walls of two bowls (30, 31); the silhouette of two high-footed bowls (36, 37), with their molded design of fishtails and waves taken directly from Chinese prototypes; and the straight sides of a small cup (33). The round form of a lime-pot (34) with its areca-vine handle is unique to Vietnam; lime-pots were part of betel-chewing paraphernalia, and their shape has not been found elsewhere in the ceramics of Southeast Asia or China.

CAT. 27

## BOWL

Tran dynasty, 13th–14th century
Glazed stoneware with two molded dragons between square-spiral design and chrysanthemum in well
3 ¾ x 9 ⅜ inches
Collection of the Art Fund, Inc. at the Birmingham Museum of Art; Bequest of William M. Spencer III AFI74.2010

**CAT. 28**

## DISH

Tran dynasty, 13th–14th century
Glazed stoneware
with two molded dragons amidst clouds
2 ¼ x 8 ¼ inches
Collection of the Art Fund, Inc. at the Birmingham Museum of Art; Bequest of William M. Spencer III
AFI158.2010

**CAT. 29**

## BOWL

Ly–Tran dynasty, 12th–13th century
Glazed stoneware with carved floral decoration on interior and carved lotus petals on exterior
4 x 8 ⅞ inches
Collection of the Art Fund, Inc. at the Birmingham Museum of Art; Bequest of William M. Spencer III
AFI53.2010

CAT. 30

## BOWL

Tran dynasty, 13th–14th century
Glazed stoneware
with carved lotus and clouds
3 1/8 x 8 inches
Collection of the Art Fund, Inc. at the
Birmingham Museum of Art; Bequest of
William M. Spencer III AFI111.2010

CAT. 31

## BOWL

Tran dynasty, 13th–14th century
Glazed stoneware with three panels of carved vegetal decoration on interior, flower in well, four carved lappets with clouds on exterior
3 1/4 x 8 1/4 inches
Collection of the Art Fund, Inc. at the Birmingham Museum of Art; Bequest of William M. Spencer III AFI155.2010

CAT. 32

## WATER DROPPER

Ly–Tran dynasty, 12th–14th century
Glazed stoneware
in the shape of a caparisoned lion
with carved lotus petal base
5 3⁄8 x 5 1⁄8 x 2 1⁄8 inches
Collection of the Art Fund, Inc. at the
Birmingham Museum of Art; Bequest of
William M. Spencer III AFI84.2010

CAT. 33

## CUP

Ly–Tran dynasty, 12th–14th century
Glazed stoneware with row of bosses
2 1⁄2 x 4 1⁄4 inches
Collection of the Art Fund, Inc. at the
Birmingham Museum of Art; Bequest of
William M. Spencer III AFI153.2010

**CAT. 34**

## LIME POT

Ly–Tran dynasty, 12th–14th century
Glazed stoneware with molded areca-plant handle
3 ¼ x 3 ½ inches
Collection of the Art Fund, Inc. at the Birmingham Museum of Art; Bequest of William M. Spencer III
AFI77.2010

INSCRIPTION

**CAT.** 35

## INCENSE BURNER

Ly–Tran dynasty, 12th–14th century
Glazed stoneware
3 ¾ x 4 ½ inches
Collection of the Art Fund, Inc. at the Birmingham Museum of Art; Bequest of William M. Spencer III AFI65.2010

CAT. 36

## BOWL

Tran dynasty, 13th–14th century
Glazed stoneware with molded design of waves and fishtails
2 ¾ x 5 ⅝ inches
Collection of the Art Fund, Inc. at the Birmingham Museum of Art; Bequest of William M. Spencer III AFI88.2010

**CAT. 37**

## BOWL

Tran dynasty, 13th–14th century
Vietnam
Glazed stoneware with molded design
of waves and fishtails
2 5⁄8 x 5 1⁄2 inches
Collection of the Art Fund, Inc. at the
Birmingham Museum of Art; Bequest of
William M. Spencer III AFI89.2010

CAT. 38

## BEAKER

Tran dynasty, 13th–14th century
Glazed stoneware
with carved lotus-petal exterior,
circle of chocolate-brown wash on base
4 ½ x 5 ⅛ inches
Collection of the Art Fund, Inc. at the
Birmingham Museum of Art; Bequest of
William M. Spencer III AFI76.2010

CAT. 39

## BOWL

Ly–Tran dynasty, 11th–13th century
Glazed stoneware, fluted sides,
kiln grit in well
3 ¼ x 5 ¾ inches
Collection of the Art Fund, Inc. at the
Birmingham Museum of Art; Bequest of
William M. Spencer III AFI98.2010

CAT. 40

# SGRAFFITO WARE

This cup is decorated in a technique known as *sgraffito,* in which a dark glaze is applied over a light-colored body and a design scratched through the glaze, revealing the light clay. An overglaze is then applied; the overglaze here is a yellow-ivory, not the transparent glaze that the potter probably intended. The row of bosses under the rim represent the nails that attach the skin of a temple drum, again suggesting that the piece was used in a religious setting.

CAT. 40

## CUP

Tran dynasty, 13th–14th century
Glazed stoneware with row of bosses
and incised scrolling floral decoration,
rim ground down
3 ¼ x 5 inches
Collection of the Art Fund, Inc. at the Birmingham
Museum of Art; Bequest of William M. Spencer III
AFI69.2010

CAT. 41–50

# OLIVE-GREEN WARES

Potters of the Ly and Tran dynasties (1009–1400) often favored an olive or brownish green glaze, the color resulting from an approximately four percent iron content in the ash-derived glaze. Many of the shapes and decorative motifs used on Vietnamese olive-glazed ceramics were taken from China, where they would have been associated with white and bluish white *(qingbai)* wares. In Vietnam, the decoration was usually applied by pressing the clay shape over a fired clay mold, rather than incising a pattern. The molded decoration of bowl (42) is a direct copy of a common Chinese Yaozhou design. A surface mark in a bowl (43) shows that its mold was cracked; the blossom is a peony, but the sharp leaves of the foliage are unlike Chinese representations of peony leaves. The small foot and straight sides of a bowl (44) form a Vietnamese, not a Chinese shape; the bowl is lop-sided but the thinness of its walls and small foot reflect skilful potting. The vegetal design on this bowl was achieved by carving the pattern into the clay surface: the glaze filled the carved areas, where the glaze became thicker, making the color of the design darker than the background.

The small marks—usually five or six—in the wells of the bowls in this grouping were the inevitable result of the pointed feet of clay rings that were placed between the stacked bowls to keep them from sticking to each other during firing. The design of a small dish (47) comprises two bands of molded chrysanthemum petals, whose outer edge forms an indented rim. An exception to the molded patterns of this group is a small beaker (48), a unique type, where five rosettes have been painted in brown iron-oxide that has run into the olive-green glaze. A water-dropper in the shape of a frog or toad (50) exemplifies the delight of the Vietnamese in the natural world.

CAT. 41

## BOWL

Ly–Tran dynasty, 12th–14th century
Glazed stoneware
with molded peony decoration
3 x 8 5/8 inches
Collection of the Art Fund, Inc. at the Birmingham Museum of Art; Bequest of William M. Spencer III AFI48.2010

CAT. 42

## BOWL

Ly–Tran dynasty, 12th–14th century
Glazed stoneware with molded chrysanthemum decoration
2 ¾ x 6 ⅞ inches
Collection of the Art Fund, Inc. at the Birmingham Museum of Art; Bequest of William M. Spencer III AFI67.2010

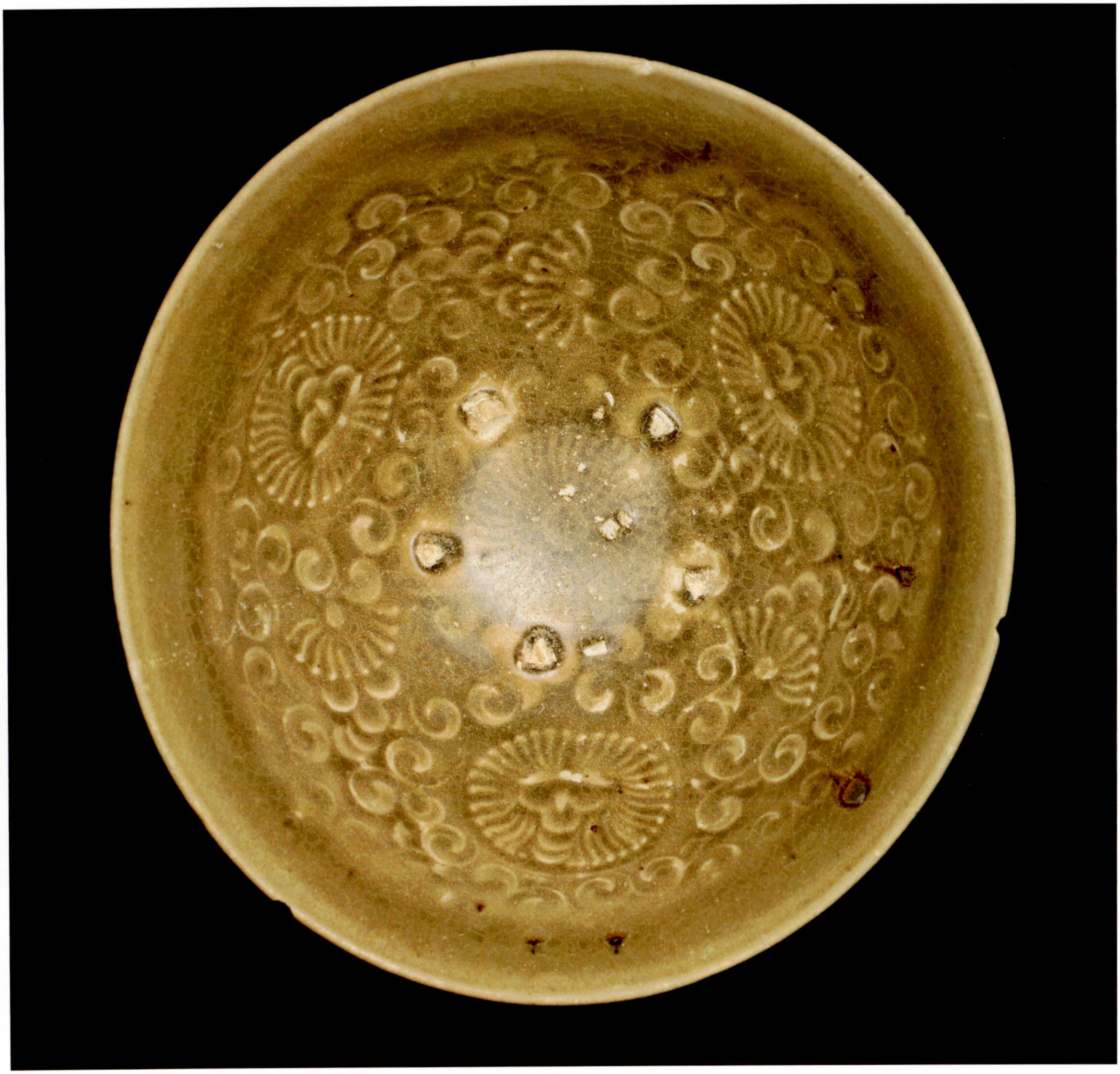

**CAT. 43**

## BOWL

Ly–Tran dynasty, 12th–14th century
Glazed stoneware
with molded peony decoration
2 7⁄8 x 7 inches
Collection of the Art Fund, Inc. at the
Birmingham Museum of Art; Bequest of
William M. Spencer III AFI102.2010

CAT. 44

## BOWL

Ly–Tran dynasty, 12th–14th century
Glazed stoneware
with carved vegetal decoration
3 ¼ x 8 inches
Collection of the Art Fund, Inc. at the Birmingham Museum of Art; Bequest of William M. Spencer III AFI56.2010

CAT. 45

## BOWL

Ly–Tran dynasty,
12th–14th century
Glazed stoneware with
molded clouds beneath
squared-spiral band
2 ¾ x 7 ⅜ inches
Collection of the Art Fund,
Inc. at the Birmingham
Museum of Art; Bequest
of William M. Spencer III
AFI119.2010

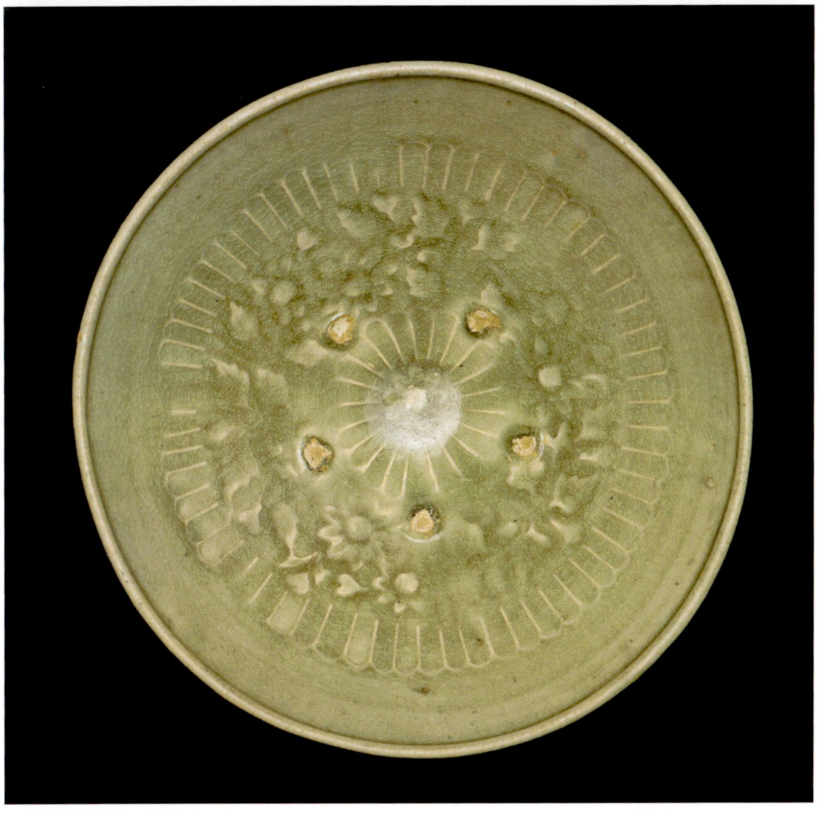

CAT. 46

## BOWL

Ly–Tran dynasty,
12th–14th century
Glazed stoneware with
molded floral decoration
beneath a molded
chrysanthemum-petal band
with chrysanthemum in well
2 3/4 x 6 5/8 inches
Collection of the Art Fund,
Inc. at the Birmingham
Museum of Art; Bequest
of William M. Spencer III
AFI93.2010

**CAT. 47**

## DISH

Tran dynasty, 13th–14th century
Glazed stoneware with two bands
of molded chrysanthemum petals
1 x 6 ½ inches
Collection of the Art Fund, Inc. at the
Birmingham Museum of Art; Bequest of
William M. Spencer III AFI73.2010

CAT. 48

## BEAKER

Tran dynasty, 13th–14th century
Glazed stoneware with five rosettes painted
in underglaze iron oxide
4 ¾ x 4 ½ inches
Collection of the Art Fund, Inc. at the Birmingham
Museum of Art; Bequest of William M. Spencer III
AFI104.2010

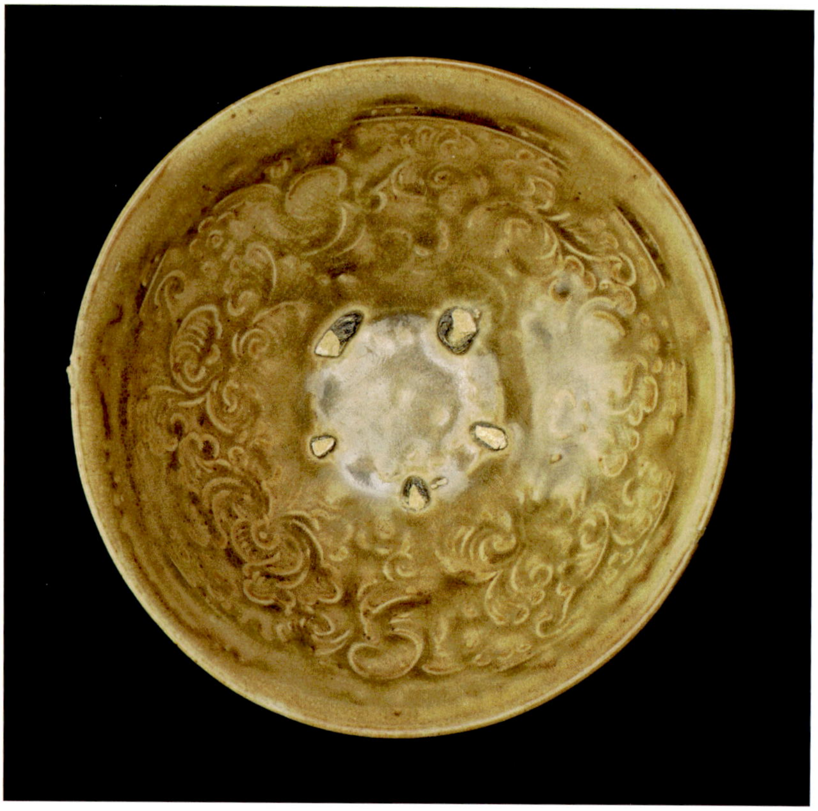

CAT. 49

## BOWL

Tran dynasty,
13th–14th century
Glazed stoneware
with molded floral decoration
2 5⁄8 x 6 3⁄4 inches
Collection of the Art Fund,
Inc. at the Birmingham
Museum of Art; Bequest
of William M. Spencer III
AFI150.2010

CAT. 50

## WATER DROPPER IN THE SHAPE OF A TOAD

15th–16th century
Glazed stoneware
3 x 4 3⁄8 inches
Gift of Dr. Robert Rosser
1977.222

**CAT.** 51–54

# OLIVE-GREEN WARES, INFANT MOTIF

A favorite decorative theme of Chinese ceramics of the Song dynasty (960–1279) showed baby boys playing among flowers, usually peony blossoms. Both motifs, baby boys and peonies, represented abundance and good fortune. The design is particularly well developed in a bowl (51) with deep olive-gray glaze, where the boys' clothes include their own little flowers and a cloudlike edge. In China this motif was usually incised, in Vietnam the motif was molded. Bowl 53 is most unusual in both the Chinese and Vietnamese traditions in that it shows three little boys rather than two. Bowl 49 shows an intermediate version of the motif, where the head and one arm can be distinguished almost as if the boys were swimming among the flowers. The straight sides of bowls 50 and 54 form a typically Vietnamese shape.

CAT. 52

## BOWL

Ly–Tran dynasty,
12th–14th century
Glazed stoneware with two
infant boys amidst peonies
2 7/8 x 7 inches
Collection of the Art Fund,
Inc. at the Birmingham
Museum of Art; Bequest
of William M. Spencer III
AFI96.2010

CAT. 51

## BOWL

Ly–Tran dynasty, 12th–14th century
Glazed stoneware with molded design
of two infant boys amidst flowers
2 ½ X 7 ⅛ inches
Collection of the Art Fund, Inc. at the Birmingham
Museum of Art; Bequest of William M. Spencer III
AFI94.2010

CAT. 53

## BOWL

Ly–Tran dynasty,
12th–14th century
Glazed stoneware with
three boys amidst flowers
3 ⅛ x 7 ¾ inches
Collection of the Art Fund, Inc. at the
Birmingham Museum of Art; Bequest of
William M. Spencer III AFI149.2010

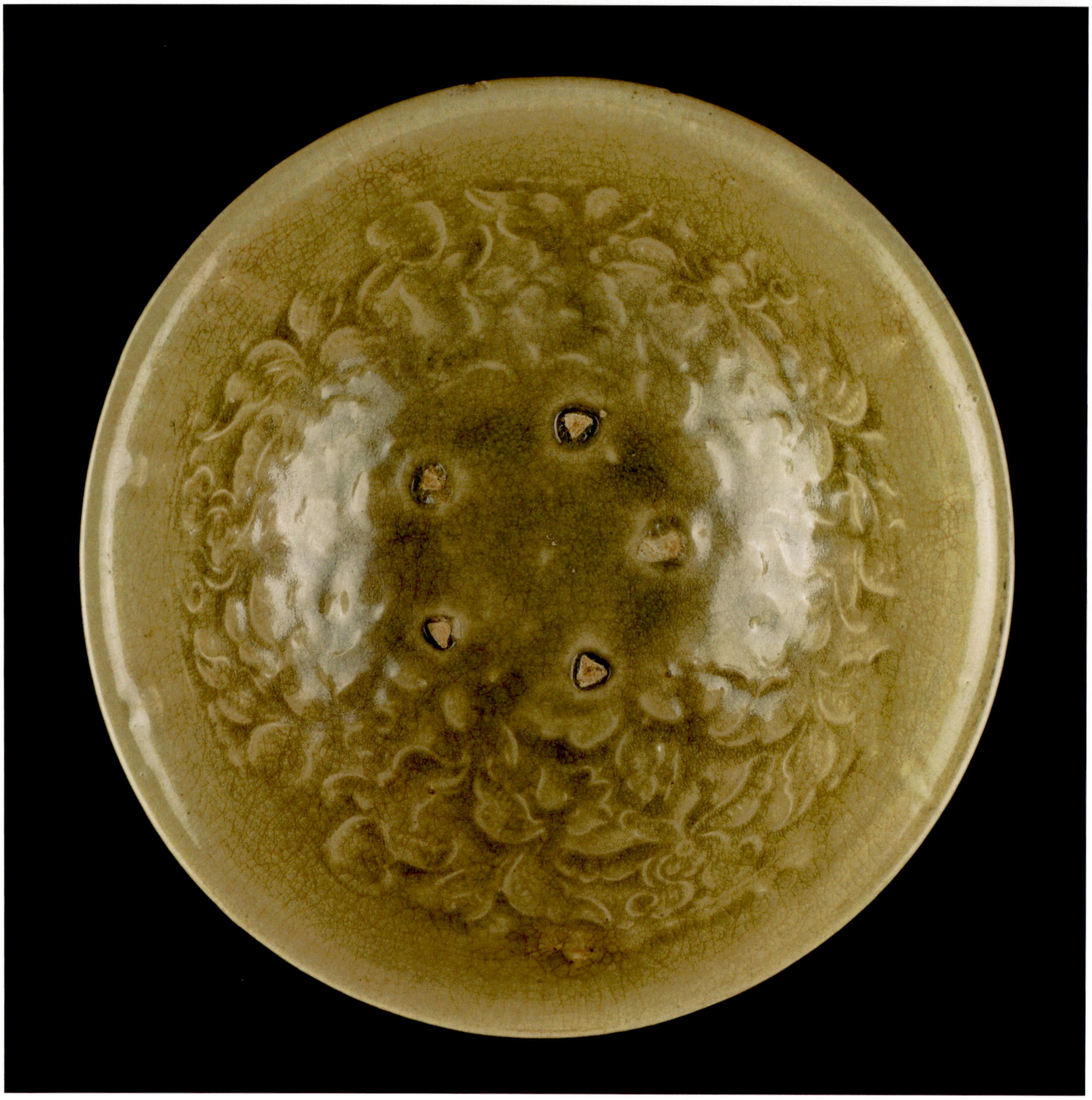

**CAT. 54**

## BOWL

Tran dynasty, 13th–14th century
Glazed stoneware with boys and flowers
3 15/16 x 7 3/8 inches
Collection of the Art Fund, Inc. at the Birmingham Museum of Art; Bequest of William M. Spencer III AFI152.2010

CAT. 55–63

# GREEN-GLAZED WARES

Vietnamese potters favored an attractive glassy green glaze that can be jewel-like where it pools. The color can range from almost yellow to a clear grasslike green. Popular shapes for this glaze included bowls with sharply inverted rims, giving a sophisticated silhouette rarely seen in China. Vietnamese covered bowls were wider than Chinese equivalents. Often these inverted bowls had complex designs carved on the inside of the well (56, 58, 59)—decoration that is not easy to achieve. Sometimes the bowls were intended to have covers, sometimes not: if glaze covers the rim, the intention was usually not to have a cover. The covers often have wavy edges, like a pie-crust or a lotus leaf.

Other shapes with this clear jewel-like green glaze include a bowl shaped like white Chinese Yuan-dynasty *shufu* bowls (61); it is decorated with under-glaze iron-brown daubs that have run into the green. Bowl 60 fits smoothly into the hands and brings to mind an alms bowl; it may have been used for receiving donations of food. Straight-sided beaker 63 bears a combined incised and combed scrolling design, and its apple-green glaze, pooling to blue, may contain copper.

**CAT. 55**

## SMALL VASE

13th–14th century
Glazed stoneware
3 x 3 ½ inches
Collection of the Art Fund, Inc. at the Birmingham Museum of Art; Bequest of William M. Spencer III AFI167.2010

**CAT. 56**

## COVERED BOWL

13th–14th century
Glazed stoneware with carved vegetal design on exterior and two flying cranes in interior
6 1/4 x 7 inches
Collection of the Art Fund, Inc. at the Birmingham Museum of Art; Bequest of William M. Spencer III
AFI58.2010a-b

**CAT. 57**

## COVERED BOWL

13th–14th century
Glazed stoneware with
carved scrolling floral decoration
5 ¾ x 6 ¾ inches
Collection of the Art Fund, Inc. at the
Birmingham Museum of Art; Bequest of
William M. Spencer III AFI163.2010a-b

CAT. 58

## BOWL

13th–14th century
Glazed stoneware with carved lotus
and arrowhead plants on interior,
floral design in well
4 1/8 x 7 3/8 inches
Collection of the Art Fund, Inc. at the
Birmingham Museum of Art; Bequest of
William M. Spencer III AFI47.2010

**CAT. 59**

## BOWL

13th–14th century
Glazed stoneware with incised scrolling design on interior, molded flower in well
3 ½ x 7 ¼ inches
Collection of the Art Fund, Inc. at the Birmingham Museum of Art; Bequest of William M. Spencer III AFI79.2010

CAT. 60

## BOWL

13th–14th century
Glazed stoneware
with carved vegetal design on exterior
4 3⁄8 x 7 1⁄4 inches
Collection of the Art Fund, Inc. at the Birmingham
Museum of Art; Bequest of William M. Spencer III
AFI50.2010

CAT. 61

## BOWL

13th–14th century
Glazed stoneware with
iron-spot "tortoiseshell" decoration
3 x 6 ½ inches
Museum purchase
2010.95

CAT. 62

## BEAKER

14th–15th century
Glazed stoneware with glaze streaks representing lotus-petals on exterior
4 1/8 x 5 1/16 inches
Gift of Dr. and Mrs. Thomas A. S. Wilson
1980.451

**CAT. 63**

## BEAKER

13th–15th century
Glazed stoneware with incised and
combed scrolling decoration, brown wash on base
5 1/8 x 4 1/2 inches
Collection of the Art Fund, Inc. at the Birmingham
Museum of Art; Bequest of William M. Spencer III
AFI125.2010

CAT. 64–69

# LONGQUAN-TYPE GREEN WARES

The iconic celadons of China are the green-glazed wares of the Longquan kilns of Zhejiang Province. The jadelike opacity of their glaze (as opposed to the jewel-like clarity of the glaze of Vietnamese green wares) is the result of innumerable tiny bubbles suspended in the thick glaze, a process that required highly controlled firing techniques. Longquan wares were admired and imported into Vietnam in antiquity—many have been found in Vietnam—and were copied by Vietnamese potters. Examples include small lotus-petal bowls, a typical Longquan style (66, 67, 68).

The opaque glazes of other Vietnamese green wares, however, may not have been intentional. Beneath the glazes of other pieces in this group, designs can be discerned: for example, lotus petals appear very faintly on the sides of covered bowl 064, and there is an incised design on the top of the rim of an incense-burner 069. If the potters had intended a thick Longquan-type glaze, made opaque by its bubbles, which would have obscured the design, they would not have gone to the trouble of creating surface designs.

A chocolate wash has been applied to the base of each of these six pieces, a unique form of decoration found on many Vietnamese ceramics dating from the beginning of the fourteenth century, perhaps earlier, to the sixteenth century. The purpose of this brown wash is not known, though there have been many conjectures; it may be relevant that the reduction firing of Longquan wares produced a brown color at the junction between the green glaze and the unglazed portion of the base, which Vietnamese potters may have wished to emulate. (In reduction firing insufficient oxygen to react with the iron-glaze is allowed into the kiln, producing green or gray-green colors rather than iron-brown or black.)

**CAT. 64**

## COVERED BOWL

13th–14th century
Glazed stoneware with
scalloped lotus-leaf cover and flanged knob
5 ¾ x 7 inches
Collection of the Art Fund, Inc. at the Birmingham
Museum of Art; Bequest of William M. Spencer III
AFI57.2010a-b

CAT. 65

## BEAKER

13th–14th century
Glazed stonewarewith
carved lotus-petal exterior,
brown wash on base
4 5⁄8 x 4 3⁄4 inches
Collection of the Art Fund, Inc. at the
Birmingham Museum of Art; Bequest of
William M. Spencer III AFI118.2010

**CAT. 66**

## BOWL

13th–14th century
Glazed stoneware with
carved lotus-petal exterior,
brown wash on base
3 x 6 inches
Collection of the Art Fund,
Inc. at the Birmingham
Museum of Art; Bequest
of William M. Spencer III
AFI131.2010

## CAT. 67

# BOWL

13th–14th century
Glazed stoneware
with carved lotus-petal exterior,
brown wash on base
3 x 6 ⅛ inches
Collection of the Art Fund, Inc. at the
Birmingham Museum of Art; Bequest of
William M. Spencer III AFI132.2010

CAT. 68

## BOWL

13th–14th century
Glazed stoneware
with carved lotus-petal exterior,
brown wash on base
2 ¾ x 6 ⅛ inches
Collection of the Art Fund, Inc. at the Birmingham Museum of Art; Bequest of William M. Spencer III AFI133.2010

CAT. 69

## INCENSE BURNER

14th century
Glazed stoneware with indented rim,
a magical multi-tailed dog seated in the well,
the hole in its head used for incense sticks,
brown wash on base
3 x 6 ½ inches
Collection of the Art Fund, Inc. at the Birmingham
Museum of Art; Bequest of William M. Spencer III
AFI95.2010

CAT. 70–74

# CERAMICS WITH BUDDHIST SYMBOLS

The Buddhist establishment was a dominant force in Vietnam. Lotuses, which grow in water and whose blossoms rise unsullied from the mud, symbolize Buddhist purity in South, East, and Southeast Asia. Lotus flowers or petals—molded, incised, carved—were an extremely common form of ceramic decoration, and a lotus pod forms the center of a brown-glazed bowl (87). A lotus motif decorating any piece of ceramic suggests that it was used in a temple or monastery setting.

The walls of two green-glazed dishes are made up of carved lotus petals surrounding a flat central portion. The character for "Great" is incised in the center of one (73), a lotus flower is incised in another (74).

Besides lotuses, some ceramics were decorated with specifically Buddhist motifs. A bowl (70) has an incised pattern of the Eight Buddhist Treasures, including an endless knot, a fish, a lotus, crossed elephant tusks, and rhinoceros horn; the last two are Vietnamese additions to the traditional eight, which originated in India. Three of six decorative panels on another bowl (84) show Treasures: a conch, the flaming jewel of Buddhist wisdom, and rhinoceros horn again. Auspicious Buddhist objects painted in underglaze iron-brown decorate a pear-shaped vase (108).

Tortoises were associated with Buddhism, and a small dish (72) has a molded tortoiseshell pattern with a tiny tortoise in the well. A bowl (71) has a molded hexagonal pattern representing tortoiseshell, with Buddhist swastikas and Daoist trigrams within the hexagonals.

The cranes, clouds, and fungus of immortality incised in the cavetto of another bowl (85) have Daoist or folk origins rather than Buddhist.

CAT. 70

## BOWL

13th–14th century
Glazed stoneware with incised decoration of eight Buddhist precious objects
3 ¼ x 8 inches
Collection of the Art Fund, Inc. at the Birmingham Museum of Art; Bequest of William M. Spencer III AFI55.2010

CAT. 71

## BOWL

13th–14th century
Glazed stoneware
with molded hexagonal design
representing tortoiseshell,
Daoist trigrams and Buddhist
swastikas in the hexagons,
a molded tortoise in the well
2 ¾ x 6 ½ inches
Collection of the Art Fund,
Inc. at the Birmingham
Museum of Art; Bequest
of William M. Spencer III
AFI66.2010

**CAT. 72**

## DISH

13th–14th century
Glazed stoneware with indented rim, molded tortoiseshell design with molded tortoise in the well, brown wash to base
1 ½ x 6 ⅛ inches
Collection of the Art Fund, Inc. at the Birmingham Museum of Art; Bequest of William M. Spencer III AFI117.2010

**CAT. 73**

## DISH

14th–15th century
Glazed stoneware with barbed rim,
row of carved chrysanthemum petals,
the character for “great” carved in the well,
brown wash on outer edge of base
1 x 6 inches
Collection of the Art Fund, Inc. at the Birmingham
Museum of Art; Bequest of William M. Spencer III
AFI82.2010

## CAT. 74

# DISH

14th–15th century
Glazed stoneware with barbed rim,
row of carved lotus petals, lotus flower at center,
brown wash on outer edge of base
1 1/8 x 6 1/8 inches
Collection of the Art Fund, Inc. at the Birmingham Museum of Art; Bequest of William M. Spencer III
AFI109.2010

CAT. 75–77

# GREEN EWERS

Three well-proportioned ewers in the Birmingham Collection have green glazes. The body of one (75) is lobed like a melon. Another (76) has a rare pear-shaped silhouette. The third (77), round-bodied, is decorated with a carved vegetal scrolling like the scrolling found on Chinese "northern celadon" wares; the glaze pooled in the carved-out areas, making the glaze thicker and therefore darker than the surrounding areas. Each ewer, used either for water or wine, has a molded spout and a small decorative handle opposite the spout: two hands, one on each side, would have been used for pouring. One ewer (76) has two more small handles, which could have been used to secure a wooden cover.

CAT. 75

## EWER

13th–14th century
Glazed stoneware with lobed body, spiral decorated spout, handle, lotus-leaf cover
7 5⁄8 x 7 inches
Collection of the Art Fund, Inc. at the Birmingham Museum of Art; Bequest of William M. Spencer III AFI42.2010a-b

**CAT. 76**

## EWER

13th–14th century
Glazed stoneware
with incised scrolling decoration,
spiral spout, four strap handles
6 ¾ x 7 ½ inches
Collection of the Art Fund, Inc. at the
Birmingham Museum of Art; Bequest of
William M. Spencer III AFI44.2010

**CAT. 77**

## EWER

13th–14th century
Glazed stoneware
with carved vegetal scrolling below
squared-spiral band and cloud whorls,
with spiral spout and ribbed handle
6 ¼ x 7 ¼ inches
Collection of the Art Fund, Inc. at the
Birmingham Museum of Art; Bequest of
William M. Spencer III AFI128.2010

CAT. 78–80

# "NAÏVE" GREEN WARES

Dragons form the principal decoration for a bowl (78), a ewer (79), and an incense-burner (80). Each is made in a vigorous naïve manner. An incised pattern of a dragon chasing a ball decorates the bowl; this round treasure, sometimes described as a "flaming pearl," is a jewel that represents Buddhist wisdom. The spout of the ewer emerges from the mouth of a bug-eyed bearded creature; its handle is made of a simple slab of clay. The incense-burner has a hollow base leading up to a bearded dragon head with a hole in an open mouth: the smoke from incense that was burned inside the hollow interior would have found its way out of the mouth and into the air.

CAT. 78

## BOWL

13th–14th century
Glazed stoneware with carved design
of dragon chasing a flaming jewel of wisdom
3 ⅞ x 7 ¼ inches
Collection of the Art Fund, Inc. at the
Birmingham Museum of Art; Bequest of
William M. Spencer III AFI97.2010

**CAT. 79**

## EWER

13th–14th century
Glazed stoneware with spout emerging from carved dragon mouth, ribbed handle
8 5⁄8 x 9 5⁄8 inches
Collection of the Art Fund, Inc. at the Birmingham Museum of Art; Bequest of William M. Spencer III AFI70.2010

**CAT. 80**

## INCENSE BURNER

13th–14th century
Glazed stoneware with hollow dragon
ascending from the well, its open mouth
allowing incense smoke to escape
4 ¼ x 7 inches
Collection of the Art Fund, Inc. at the
Birmingham Museum of Art; Bequest of
William M. Spencer III AFI164.2010

CAT. 81–88

# SMALL-FOOTED BOWLS WITH NOTCHED EVERTED RIMS

When bowls were stacked for firing in Vietnamese kilns, a doughnut-shaped ring of clay was often placed in the well of each bowl to prevent it from fusing with its neighbors during firing. After the glaze on the bowl had been applied and was still viscous, a circle of glaze in the well of the bowl would be scraped away with a bamboo scraper, so that no glaze touched the divider. Sometimes the rings had little feet (usually five or six); in this case no glaze was scraped away, but small spurmarks would be left in the bottom of the well. The alternative was to place each bowl in a separate clay "box," called a saggar, an expensive process that reduced the number of pieces that could be fitted into the kiln. The Chinese used saggars more than the Vietnamese did, to avoid blemishes like spurmarks and unglazed rings.

Bowls with low, small foot-rings and notched everted rims were common Vietnamese products of the fourteenth and fifteenth centuries. They were extensively exported to Indonesia and the Philippines. Common glaze colors for these bowls include olive-green, clear grass-green, chocolate-brown, and ivory. Often the bowls bear molded or incised decorations in the cavetto; the decoration of bowl 84 gives us a glimpse of what people wore at the time, robes and tunics. The notching in the rim sometimes suggests lotus petals.

CAT. 81

## BOWL

14th–15th century
Glazed stoneware with notched rim and molded floral decoration
2 5⁄8 x 6 3⁄8 inches
Collection of the Art Fund, Inc. at the Birmingham Museum of Art; Bequest of William M. Spencer III
AFI172.2010

## CAT. 82

# BOWL

14th–15th century
Glazed stoneware with
molded vegetal decoration and moon
2 5⁄8 x 6 1⁄4 inches
Collection of the Art Fund, Inc. at the
Birmingham Museum of Art; Bequest of
William M. Spencer III AFI175.2010

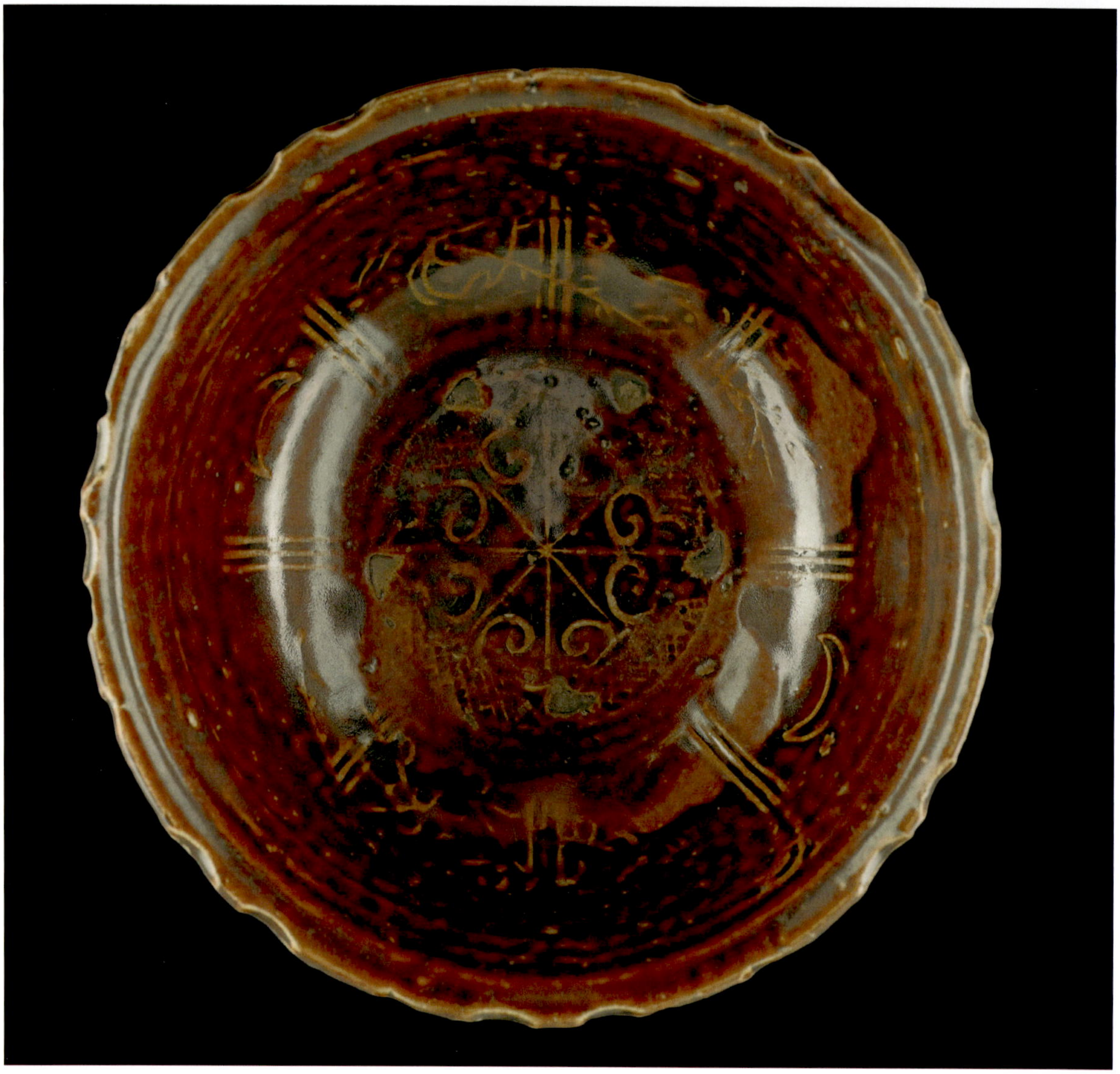

**CAT.** 83

# BOWL

14th–15th century
Glazed stoneware
with molded cloud design
2 ⅜ x 6 ½ inches
Collection of the Art Fund, Inc. at the Birmingham Museum of Art; Bequest of William M. Spencer III AFI99.2010

**CAT. 84**

## BOWL

14th–15th century
Glazed stoneware with molded design
of three human figures alternating with
three of the eight Buddhist precious objects,
the characters *guanyao* "official ware" at center
2 ½ x 6 ¼ inches
Collection of the Art Fund, Inc. at the Birmingham
Museum of Art; Bequest of William M. Spencer III
AFI64.2010

CAT. 85

## BOWL

14th–15th century
Glazed stoneware with barbed rim, molded design of cranes, fungus of immortality, clouds, and lotus blossoms in eight panels, light brown wash to base
2 7/8 x 6 1/2 inches
Collection of the Art Fund, Inc. at the Birmingham Museum of Art; Bequest of William M. Spencer III AFI63.2010

CAT. 86

## BOWL

14th–15th century
Glazed stoneware
with notched rim,
incised lotus-blossoms in
five panels, apple-green glaze,
brown wash to base
2 ⅝ x 6 ½ inches
Collection of the Art Fund,
Inc. at the Birmingham
Museum of Art; Bequest
of William M. Spencer III
AFI90.2010

CAT. 87

## BOWL

14th–15th century
Glazed stoneware with molded floral designs, lotus pod in the well
2 5⁄8 x 6 5⁄8 inches
Collection of the Art Fund, Inc. at the Birmingham Museum of Art; Bequest of William M. Spencer III AFI103.2010

CAT. 88

## BOWL

14th–15th century
Glazed stoneware with notched rim, molded design of alternating floral and cloud designs, cloud motifs in the well
2 ⅜ x 6 ½ inches
Collection of the Art Fund, Inc. at the Birmingham Museum of Art; Bequest of William M. Spencer III AFI126.2010

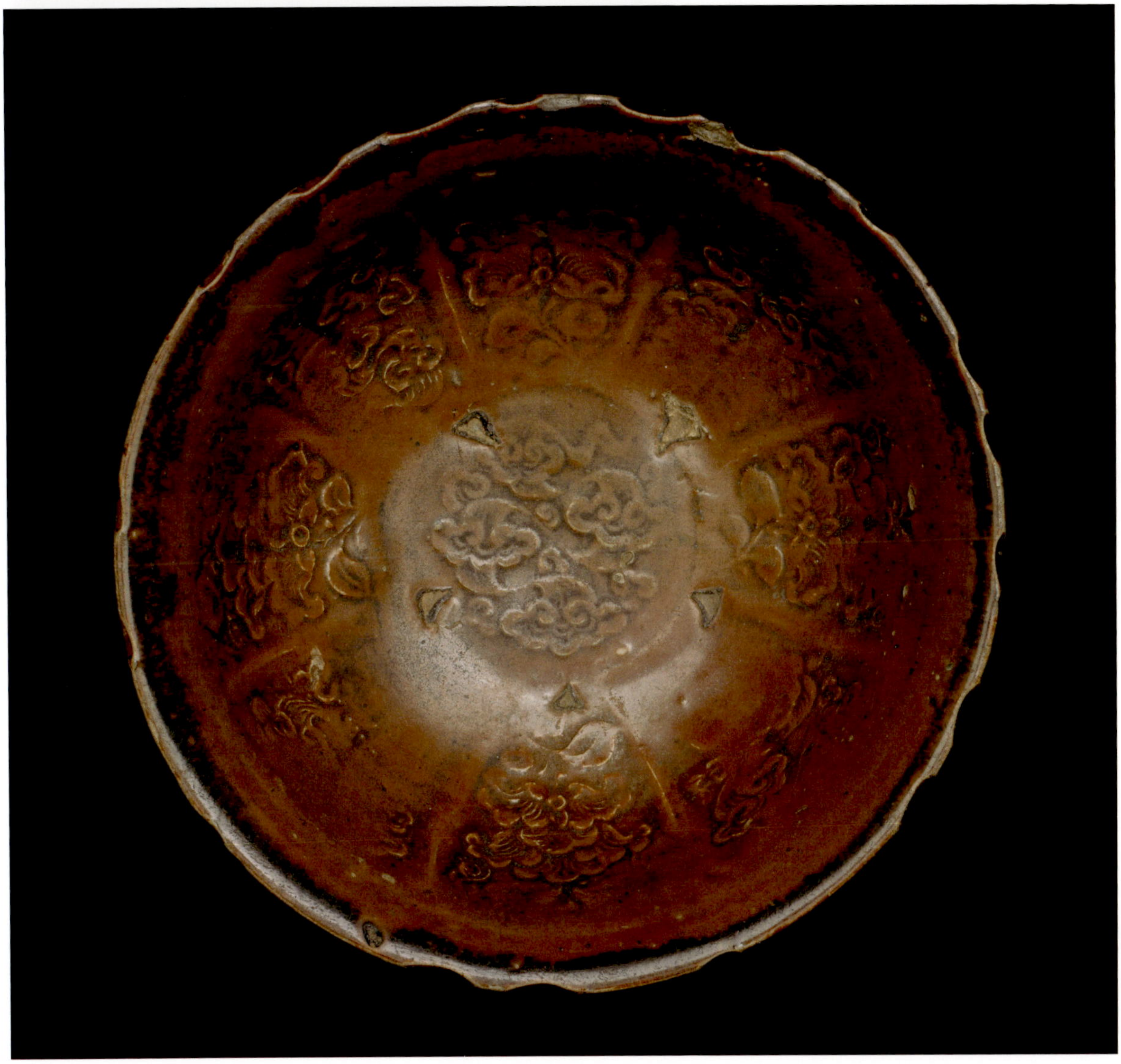

CAT. 89–96

# BROWN WARES

Deep chocolate-brown glazes derived from iron-oxide, the same glazes as were used in earlier ceramics with inlaid designs (17–22), were popular during the fourteenth to sixteenth centuries. A small vase (90) has a thick brown glaze of a type treasured in China and Japan for tea-bowls. In Japan the glaze is known as *temmoku,* after the name of a temple in southern China where dark-colored iron-glazed bowls were used for drinking tea. The glaze of the vase here, where iron crystals have been precipitated out through a long firing and slow cooling process, is particularly thick and luxurious. Another specialized process can be seen in a bowl (95) where daubs of yellow glaze made from straw-ash have been applied to the exterior to suggest tortoiseshell.

Vessels glazed brown on the outside were often glazed white or ivory on the inside in Vietnam, a pleasing contrast (90–94, 96). Two such bowls (92, 93) have a molded floral pattern in the well.

CAT. 89

## BOWL

14th–15th century
Glazed stoneware
with molded decoration,
lotus pod in the well
2 ½ x 6 ¾ inches
Gift of Dr. and Mrs. Richard H. Cord
1976.314

## CAT. 90

# VASE

12th–14th century
Glazed stoneware,
flaring mouth, thick temmoku
"hare's fur" glaze on exterior
4 x 5 inches
Collection of the Art Fund, Inc. at the
Birmingham Museum of Art; Bequest of
William M. Spencer III AFI86.2010

## CAT. 91

# INCENSE BURNER

14th–15th century
Glazed stoneware, green-white glaze
on interior (rim ground down)
6 5/8 x 7 1/4 inches
Collection of the Art Fund, Inc. at the
Birmingham Museum of Art; Bequest of
William M. Spencer III AFI45.2010

**CAT. 92**

## BOWL

12th–14th century
Glazed stoneware with
molded floral decoration,
ivory glaze in well
2 ½ x 6 ¼ inches
Collection of the Art Fund,
Inc. at the Birmingham
Museum of Art; Bequest
of William M. Spencer III
AF136.2010

CAT. 93

## BOWL

12th–14th century
Glazed stoneware with molded floral decoration, ivory glaze in well
2 ½ x 6 ¼ inches
Collection of the Art Fund, Inc. at the Birmingham Museum of Art; Bequest of William M. Spencer III
AFI137.2010

## CAT. 94

# EWER

14th–15th century
Glazed stoneware with
molded rosette decoration
in place of handle
6 5⁄8 x 6 1⁄8 inches
Collection of the Art Fund,
Inc. at the Birmingham
Museum of Art; Bequest
of William M. Spencer III
AFI91.2010

## CAT. 95

# BOWL

13th–14th century
Glazed stoneware with
yellow-daub straw-ash glaze
"tortoiseshell" decoration
2 5⁄8 x 6 1⁄4 inches
Collection of the Art Fund,
Inc. at the Birmingham
Museum of Art; Bequest
of William M. Spencer III
AFI101.2010

CAT. 96

## BOWL

14th–15th century
Glazed stoneware, ivory glaze in well
2 ¾ x 7 ⅛ inches
Collection of the Art Fund, Inc. at the Birmingham Museum of Art; Bequest of William M. Spencer III AFI129.2010

CAT. 97–102

# EARLY UNDERGLAZE-BROWN WARES

A major development in the decoration of Chinese and Vietnamese ceramics was the painting of designs on a white-slipped body; a transparent glaze was then applied over the whole and the piece fired. Ceramics with this form of decoration became immensely popular, forming the basis for a vast trade network stretching from China and Vietnam to the Middle East to Indonesia and the Philippines. Vietnamese ceramics have for centuries been associated with underglaze-decorated types.

In Vietnam underglaze cobalt-blue decoration seems to have been preceded by underglaze brown iron-oxide painting. The most common motif on early Vietnamese bowls with underglaze-brown painting was a loose, almost calligraphic daisy or chrysanthemum spray in the well (110, 113). Sherds with this decoration found in Japanese temple excavations appear to be datable to as early as the second quarter of the fourteenth century. In Vietnam this form of decoration may have been preceded by even simpler designs, quick floral daubs like those we see on bowls 97 to 102.

CAT. 97

## COVERED BOWL

13th–14th century
Glazed stoneware with domed lid,
floral shapes painted in underglaze-iron,
potter's mark on base
5 5⁄8 x 7 1⁄4 inches
Collection of the Art Fund, Inc. at the
Birmingham Museum of Art; Bequest of
William M. Spencer III AFI112.2010a-b

CAT. 98

## BOWL

13th–14th century
Glazed stoneware
with daubs of brown underglaze-iron
2 ¾ x 5 ⅞ inches
Collection of the Art Fund, Inc. at the
Birmingham Museum of Art; Bequest of
William M. Spencer III AFI121.2010

## CAT. 99

# BOWL

13th–14th century
Glazed stoneware
with floral shapes painted
in underglaze-iron
2 x 4 ⅞ inches
Collection of the Art Fund, Inc. at the Birmingham Museum of Art; Bequest of William M. Spencer III
AFI122.2010

## CAT. 100

# BOWL

13th–14th century
Glazed stoneware
with floral shapes painted
in underglaze-iron
3 ⅜ x 6 ½ inches
Collection of the Art Fund, Inc. at the Birmingham Museum of Art; Bequest of William M. Spencer III
AFI123.2010

CAT. 101

## BOWL

13th–14th century
Glazed stoneware with
floral shapes painted in underglaze-iron
(this bowl originally had a cover)
3 ½ x 7 ½ inches
Collection of the Art Fund, Inc. at the
Birmingham Museum of Art; Bequest of
William M. Spencer III AFI156.2010

**CAT. 102**

## BOWL

13th–14th century
Glazed stoneware, scalloped rim,
loose floral shapes painted in underglaze-iron
3 1/4 x 7 1/2 inches
Collection of the Art Fund, Inc. at the Birmingham
Museum of Art; Bequest of William M. Spencer III
AFI46.2010

CAT. 103–109

# UNDERGLAZE-BROWN WARES

The quickly drawn underglaze-iron daubs we see in the previous group developed into clearly defined floral sprays, scrolling, and other motifs. Floral sprays decorate three ewers (103–105); one of the ewers is lobed like a melon, and two have round bulbous bodies, a typical Vietnamese ewer shape. In each, we can see how a white slip was applied to provide a smooth white surface for painting the decoration.

Two beakers bear scrolling iron-brown designs reminiscent of clouds rather than flowers (106, 107). More formal lotus designs decorate two *yuhuchun*-shaped vases; one has banana-leaf designs (109), the other Buddhist symbols (108).

## CAT. 103

# BULBOUS EWER

13th–14th century
Glazed stoneware with flat-topped cover, molded spout, spiral handle, floral designs painted in underglaze-iron
6 ½ x 6 inches
Collection of the Art Fund, Inc. at the Birmingham Museum of Art; Bequest of William M. Spencer III AFI157.2010a-b

INSCRIPTION

**CAT. 104**

## BULBOUS EWER

13th–14th century
Glazed stoneware with flat-topped cover, molded spout, spiral handle, floral designs painted in underglaze-iron
7 1/4 x 6 7/8 inches
Collection of the Art Fund, Inc. at the Birmingham Museum of Art; Bequest of William M. Spencer III AFI52.2010a-b

**CAT. 105**

## MELON EWER

13th–14th century
Glazed stoneware, lobed body,
domed cover with vegetal sprig handle,
molded spout, spiral handle, floral sprays
painted in underglaze-iron
7 5⁄8 x 6 1⁄2 inches
Collection of the Art Fund, Inc. at the
Birmingham Museum of Art; Bequest of
William M. Spencer III AFI38.2010a-b

**CAT. 106**

## BEAKER

14th century
Glazed stoneware with scrolling sprays
painted in underglaze-iron
5 9⁄16 x 4 1⁄8 inches
Gift of Mr. and Mrs. Harris Saunders Jr.
1980.426

CAT. 107

## BEAKER

14th century
Glazed stoneware with scrolling sprays painted in underglaze-iron
5 x 5 ½ inches
Collection of the Art Fund, Inc. at the Birmingham Museum of Art; Bequest of William M. Spencer III AFI80.2010

CAT. 108

## *YUHUCHUN* BOTTLE

14th century
Glazed stoneware, scrolling lotus designs on body with four of the eight Buddhist precious symbols, plantain leaves below rim, all painted in underglaze-iron
11 x 5 ¾ inches
Gift of Dr. and Mrs. Orville W. Clayton
1980.393

CAT. 109

## *YUHUCHUN* BOTTLE

14th–15th century
Glazed stoneware with scrolling lotus designs, grasses and plants below rim, all painted in underglaze-iron
10 ⅜ x 6 inches
Collection of the Art Fund, Inc. at the Birmingham Museum of Art; Bequest of William M. Spencer III
AFI169.2010

CAT. 110–114

# DEVELOPMENT OF COBALT-BLUE UNDERGLAZE PAINTING

The most common examples of Vietnamese underglaze iron-brown painting are bowls decorated with a loosely drawn floral spray showing a daisy or chrysanthemum in the well. A simple scrolling band between two lines appears under the interior rim, with a wider scrolling band between two lines on the exterior (like the cloud scrolls of beakers 106 and 107). Vietnamese bowls of this type have been found widely within Vietnam and in other parts of Southeast Asia, especially the Philippines and Indonesia, where they formed part of an established export trade in ceramics. These underglaze-painted bowls augmented trade in bowls with molded and incised designs like 81 to 88.

Blue cobalt-oxide must have been considered a more attractive color and became increasingly popular, superseding brown iron-oxide. Two bowls (112 and 113) show intermediate stages, in which the floral sprays and scrolling have been painted in a low-grade blue-brown cobalt and the enclosing lines have been painted in brown iron-oxide. In its final form the whole design was painted in bright blue cobalt-oxide.

CAT. 110

## BOWL

14th century
Glazed stoneware with chrysanthemum spray in well and scrolling bands below exterior rim, painted in underglaze-iron
2 x 5 ½ inches
Gift of Mr. William M. Spencer III
1977.233

CAT. 111

## BOWL

14th century
Glazed stoneware with chrysanthemum spray in well and scrolling bands below exterior rim, painted in underglaze-iron
3 1/4 x 7 5/8 inches
Collection of the Art Fund, Inc. at the Birmingham Museum of Art; Bequest of William M. Spencer III AFI59.2010

CAT. 112

## BOWL

14th century
Glazed stoneware with chrysanthemum spray in well and scrolling bands below rim painted in blue-brown cobalt-oxide, with enclosing lines in brown iron-oxide
3 x 6 ½ inches
Collection of the Art Fund, Inc. at the Birmingham Museum of Art; Bequest of William M. Spencer III AFI60.2010

CAT. 113

## BOWL

14th century
Glazed stoneware
with chrysanthemum spray
in well and scrolling band
below rim painted in blue-
brown oxide, with enclosing
lines in brown iron-oxide
2 7/8 x 6 3/4 inches
Collection of the Art Fund,
Inc. at the Birmingham
Museum of Art; Bequest
of William M. Spencer III
AFI87.2010

CAT. 114

## DISH

14th century
Glazed stoneware with chrysanthemum spray in well and band below rim painted in blue cobalt-oxide, circles painted in low-grade brownish cobalt-oxide
2 ½ x 10 ¾ inches
Gift of Mr. and Mrs. Paul Kassouf 1976.320

CAT. 115–119

# UNDERGLAZE BLUE

Dishes and vessels of all sorts with underglaze-blue designs became immensely popular in China during the fourteenth and fifteenth centuries, and were exported all over Asia. Using the same techniques, Vietnamese potters developed their own designs. Favorite motifs were flower sprays, especially lotuses, peonies, and chrysanthemums, all auspicious symbols (115–117); also fish, birds, and other themes from nature, sometimes dragons. The painting on Vietnamese blue-and-whites is usually much more free than the designs on Chinese blue-and-whites; the lively deer of dish 118 is a good example. An informal motif that would never be found on a Chinese dish shows mating birds, a sign of fecundity; also shrimp, a Vietnamese food staple.

In the mid-fifteenth century Ming China withdrew from the export trade. Vietnamese potters quickly filled the void, shipping substantial quantities of large dishes and a wide variety of other shapes to Iran, Egypt, Indonesia, and other Islamic countries, where large fine serving dishes were appropriate for eating customs. Some of these fine ceramics have been documented in imperial Middle Eastern collections for centuries.

**CAT. 115**

## DISH

15th century
Glazed stoneware with
chrysanthemums and cloud patterns in well,
floral scrolling below rim and scrolling on rim,
all painted in underglaze-blue cobalt-oxide
3 1/8 x 14 5/8 inches
Gift of Mr. and Mrs. James T. Stephens 1984.36

CAT. 116

## DISH

15th–16th century
Glazed stoneware with lotus flower in center surrounded by band of lotus petals, floral meanders and scrolling on rim, lappets on exterior, all painted in underglaze-blue cobalt-oxide
3 1/8 x 13 3/4 inches
Gift of Mr. and Mrs. Harris Saunders, Jr. 1980.427

CAT. 117

## DISH

15th–16th century
Glazed stoneware with chrysanthemum in center
surrounded by scrolling clouds, scroll pattern on rim,
all painted in underglaze-blue cobalt-oxide
2 1/4 x 10 inches
Gift of Dr. Chandler H. and Jane Paris Smith 1978.92

CAT. 118

## DISH

15th–16th century
Glazed stoneware with deer by a river with pine, bamboo, and orchid plants surrounded by a band of scalloped lotus petals, chrysanthemum sprays on cavetto, lappets on exterior, all painted in underglaze-blue cobalt-oxide
3 x 14 5⁄8 inches
Gift of Mr. and Mrs. Paul Kassouf 1980.411

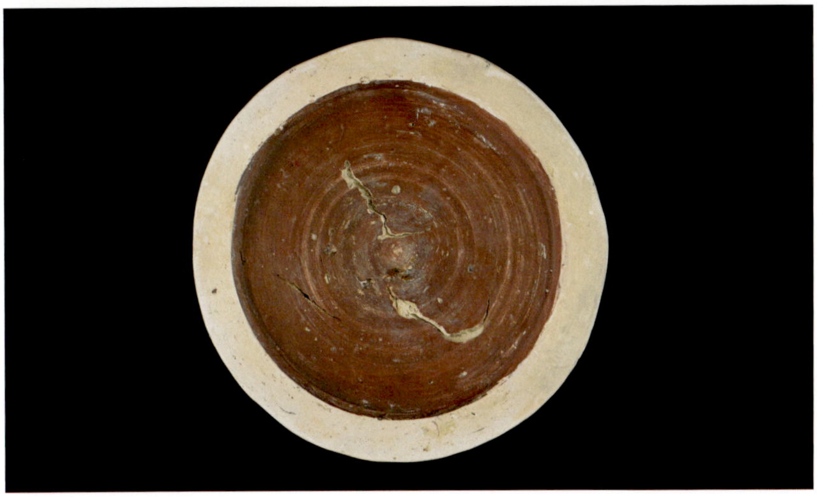

CAT. 119

## JAR

15th–16th century
Glazed stoneware with six Needlefish (family Belonidae) swimming amidst waterweeds, lotus-petal collar, lappets above base, all painted in underglaze-blue cobalt-oxide
12 3⁄16 x 8 1⁄4 inches
Gift of Mr. and Mrs. Bartlett B. Bretz 1977.247

CAT. 120–121

# UNDERGLAZE BLUE WITH OVERGLAZE ENAMELS

The decoration of dishes and other vessels painted with the popular blue pigments became even more lavish with the development of overglaze painting. After firing, a piece with underglaze-blue painting would be enhanced with overglaze decoration. Colored enamels, red, green, and occasionally yellow, would be applied, and the piece re-fired at a lower temperature. Being less highly fired, these overglaze enamels were easily abraded, but when freshly manufactured these colorful pieces must have been stunning, and they figured large in the export trade.

Birmingham's collection includes two rare pieces of this type. One is a dish showing figures in a landscape (120); human figures were not often used as design motifs in Vietnamese ceramics. The other is a highly ornate jar painted with mythical animals: two winged horses and two tiger-like creatures, one with a demon's head (121). The jar is further adorned with four monster masks under the rim and four unglazed openwork panels on the shoulders in the form of cranes and clouds. This extraordinary ceramic is unique in its large size, fine painting, and the complexity and sophistication of its construction and decoration.

CAT. 120

## DISH

15th–16th century
Glazed stoneware with scalloped rim, design of figures in a landscape surrounded by floral band painted in underglaze-blue cobalt-oxide and overglaze red and green enamels
2 7⁄8 x 13 7⁄8 inches
Gift of Mr. and Mrs. Elton B. Stephens 1978.183

**CAT.** 121

## JAR

16th century
Glazed stoneware with four monster-head bosses below rim, mythological animals with cloud and flame motifs finely painted in underglaze-blue cobalt-oxide and overglaze enamels, with inset, reticulated, bisque-fired roundels with cranes
24 1/4 x 15 inches
Collection of the Art Fund, Inc. at the Birmingham Museum of Art; Purchase with funds provided by the Estate of William M. Spencer III AFI289.2010

CAT. 122–127

# UNDERGLAZE-BLUE CERAMICS FOR TEMPLE USE

Underglaze-blue painted ceramics were as popular in Buddhist temples as they were for domestic use. A bowl (122) is decorated with a double-*vajra,* an Esoteric Buddhist ritual implement representing a thunderbolt. Specific ceramic shapes were developed for temple use, such as a stand for offerings of fruit called a *qua bong* (123). A large wide bowl with three legs is a temple incense-burner (124). Bulbous vessels, known as *kendi* in Southeast Asia *(kundika* in Sanskrit), were used for sprinkling holy water for purification; Birmingham has three examples, one with unusual and well-painted human figures in a garden (125), one with a gold collar, probably added in Indonesia (126), and one with overglaze enamels (127).

CAT. 122

## BOWL

16th century
Glazed stoneware with double-vajra in well, surrounded by lotus-flower meanders, leaves, crosshatch pattern around rim, two mythical animals cavort amidst scrolling lotus flowers and ferns on exterior, painted in underglaze-blue cobalt-oxide.
9 x 3 ⅞ inches
Gift of Dr. and Mrs. Charles B. Crow
1976.317

CAT. 123

## OFFERING STAND

15th–16th century
Glazed stoneware with peony spray in center of bowl surrounded by auspicious Buddhist symbols, floral meanders on exterior, band of lotus petals below waist, cloud and floral motifs on base, painted in underglaze-blue cobalt-oxide
8 1/4 x 11 1/2 inches
Museum purchase 1975.5

**CAT. 124**

## INCENSE BURNER

15th century
Glazed stoneware with scrolling lotus flowers, scroll pattern around neck, diaper band below rim on interior, three animal-shaped feet, painted in underglaze-blue cobalt- oxide
4 1/2 x 11 1/8 inches
Collection of the Art Fund, Inc. at the Birmingham Museum of Art; Bequest of William M. Spencer III AFI61.2010

CAT. 125

## KENDI

15th century
Glazed stoneware with panels with figures and pine trees, floral sprays and flaming jewels on spout and band of lotus petals around neck, painted in underglaze-blue cobalt-oxide
5 x 7 5/8 inches
Gift of Mr. Elton B. Stephens 1978.184

CAT. 126

## KENDI

16th century
Glazed stoneware with gold collar, two fish swimming amidst scrolling patterns painted in underglaze-blue cobalt-oxide, water plants painted in deteriorated overglaze enamels
5 1/2 x 5 15/16 inches
Gift of Mr. and Mrs. Harris Saunders, Jr. 1980.425

**CAT. 127**

## KENDI

16th century
Glazed stoneware with scrolling floral patterns, six lappets below neck, all painted in underglaze-blue cobalt-oxide and overglaze enamels
6 7/8 x 5 1/4 inches
Gift of Mr. and Mrs. Paul Kassouf 1980.410

CAT. 128–130

# HOI-AN

The study of ancient ceramics worldwide has been revolutionized in recent decades by the discovery of shipwrecks containing thousands, sometimes hundreds of thousands, of pieces. The most significant discovery for the study of Vietnamese ceramics has been a wreck that sank off Hoi-An, near Danang, at the end of the fifteenth century from which a quarter of a million blue-and-white pieces have been recovered. The objects found in a shipwreck form a sort of time capsule, and the Hoi-An pieces covered a very wide range of types that we now know must have all been made in the same period. Many of the pieces were auctioned in San Francisco in the year 2000 with the approval of the Vietnamese government. Birmingham Museum of Art purchased a fine dish with a mythological animal design (128), two sets of bowls in the shape of parrots (129, 130), a well-loved motif, and a set of wine cups with brown exterior and white interior with the character for “good luck” painted in blue in the well (144).

**CAT. 128**

## DISH

15th–16th century
Glazed stoneware with mythical beast in center surrounded by *ruyi*-headed clouds, jeweled lappets on exterior, painted in underglaze-blue cobalt-oxide
2 7⁄8 x 14 1⁄4 inches
Museum purchase with funds from the Endowed Funds for Acquisitions 2000.111

## CAT. 129

# PARROT-SHAPED BOWLS

15th–16th century
Glazed stoneware with leaf decoration on exterior and details on birds painted in underglaze-blue cobalt-oxide
3 ½ x 3 ¼ inches (each)
Museum purchase with funds from the Endowed Funds for Acquisitions 2000.112.1-.5

**CAT. 130**

## PARROT-SHAPED BOWLS

15th–16th century
Glazed stoneware with details of birds and a leaf in the well of each bowl painted in underglaze-blue cobalt-oxide and overglaze red and green enamels
4 x 3 3⁄8 inches (each)
Museum purchase with funds from the Endowed Funds for Acquisitions 2000.113.1-.5

CAT. 131–145

# UNDERGLAZE BLUE, EVERYDAY OBJECTS

When China renewed its export trade, fine Vietnamese blue-and-white ceramics were largely squeezed out of the export markets, but large numbers of small blue-and-white ceramics continued to be made for domestic use. Some pieces were well made and carefully decorated (132, 133) but generally the quality of Vietnamese design and manufacture declined over the course of the sixteenth century. For example, the painting of a sixteenth-century jar (143) does not compare with the lively fish that decorate an earlier jar (119). Small items such as water-droppers, used for mixing ink when writing with a brush, were made in charming and imaginative shapes (136, 137). Covered boxes were popular (138, 139). A style of high-footed bowl, probably for food, became common—some were imported into Japan, where they were treasured as tea-bowls and listed in contemporary collections of tea-wares.

**CAT. 131**

## BOWL

15th–16th century
Glazed stoneware with silver rim, peony sprays, lotus-petal collar above and lappets below, painted in underglaze-blue cobalt-oxide
10 1⁄8 x 6 7⁄8 inches
Gift of Mr. and Mrs. James T. Stephens 1978.180

**CAT. 132**

## SMALL EWER

15th–16th century
Glazed stoneware with *ruyi* cloud panels below lotus-petal collar and above panels with Buddhist *cintāmani* jewels, painted in underglaze-blue cobalt-oxide
6 7/8 x 5 5/16 inches
Gift of Mr. and Mrs. Paul Kassouf
1980.409

CAT. 133

## BOWL

15th–16th century
Glazed stoneware with scrolling peonies, a squared-spiral scrolling pattern above and lappets below, painted in underglaze-blue cobalt-oxide
5 x 7 3/8 inches
Gift of Dr. Chandler H. and Jane Paris Smith 1980.435

CAT. 134

## BOWL

16th century
Glazed stoneware with floral meanders, a scrolling pattern above and lotus petals below, painted in underglaze-blue cobalt-oxide
3 x 4 3/16 inches
Gift of Dr. and Mrs. John D. Elmore 1980.400

**CAT. 135**

## BOTTLE

15th–16th century
Glazed stoneware, blue cobalt glaze, silver repair to neck
4 1/2 x 9 1/8 inches
Gift of Dr. and Mrs. Lawrence J. Lemak 1980.413

**CAT. 136**

## WATER DROPPER IN THE SHAPE OF A TORTOISE

15th–16th century
Glazed stoneware, painted in
underglaze-blue cobalt-oxide
1 3⁄8 x 3 inches
Gift of Mr. and Mrs. Thomas E. Rast
1978.86

**CAT. 137**

## WATER DROPPER IN THE SHAPE OF TWO MANDARIN DUCKS

15th–16th century
Glazed stoneware painted in
underglaze-blue cobalt-oxide
4 ½ x 5 inches
Gift of Dr. and Mrs. Chester C. Brummett 1976.310

CAT. 138

## COVERED BOX

16th century
Glazed stoneware with chrysanthemum on cover, floral sprays on side, painted in underglaze-blue cobalt-oxide
4 x 3 inches
Gift of Dr. and Mrs. Sheridan W. Shirley
1976.330a-b

CAT. 139

## COVERED BOX

15th–16th century
Glazed stoneware with floral and trellis patterns set in panels painted in underglaze-blue cobalt-oxide and overglaze enamels
4 x 3 inches
Gift of Dr. and Mrs. L. Clark Gravlee
1976.338a-b

CAT. 140

## COVERED JAR

16th century
Glazed stoneware with floral spray on top, panels showing plants on side, lappets below, painted in underglaze-blue cobalt-oxide
5 x 4 inches
Collection of the Art Fund, Inc. at the Birmingham Museum of Art; Bequest of William M. Spencer III AFI181.2010a-b

**CAT. 141**

## HIGH-FOOTED BOWL

15th–16th century
Glazed stoneware with the character phuc, "good fortune," in well, floral meander on rim, chrysanthemum sprays, painted in underglaze-blue cobalt-oxide
3 ½ x 5 ¼ inches
Collection of the Art Fund, Inc. at the Birmingham Museum of Art; Bequest of William M. Spencer III
AFI180.2010

**CAT. 142**

## HIGH-FOOTED BOWL

16th century
Glazed stoneware with vegetal sprays, chrysanthemums, and lappets painted in underglaze-blue cobalt-oxide, brown wash on base
3 5⁄8 x 5 7⁄8 inches
Collection of the Art Fund, Inc. at the Birmingham Museum of Art; Bequest of William M. Spencer III
AFI127.2010

**CAT. 143**

## JAR

16th century
Glazed stoneware with four loop handles, lappets with stylized floral patterns below rim, floral meanders on upper half of body, painted in underglaze-blue cobalt-oxide
7 ¼ x 5 ⅞ inches
Gift of Dr. and Mrs. John D. Elmore 1978.79

CAT. 144

## WINE CUPS

15th–16th century
Glazed stoneware, brown exterior, white interior, the character phuc, “good fortune,” painted in well in underglaze-blue cobalt-oxide
2 x 2 7/8 inches (each)
Museum purchase with funds from the Endowed Funds for Acquisitions 2000.114.1-.5

CAT. 145

## WINE CUP

16th century
Glazed stoneware with brown cross-hatched exterior, white interior, the character phuc, "good fortune," painted in underglaze cobalt blue-oxide
2 1⁄8 x 3 5⁄8 inches
Collection of the Art Fund, Inc. at the Birmingham Museum of Art; Bequest of William M. Spencer III AFI116.2010

CAT. 146–153

# LATER WHITE WARES

Elegant shapes continued to be made in white-slipped forms, either plain or with a single decorative circle of underglaze blue. A covered jar (146) is interesting in that it rings like porcelain when struck, though Vietnam did not have the clay to make true porcelain. Without such clay, Vietnamese ceramics are stoneware, though Vietnamese potters achieved kiln temperatures high enough to make porcelain. A lime-pot (153) is a shape unique to Vietnam. These lime-pots were containers for the lime that was an essential part of the paraphernalia associated with the chewing of areca nuts wrapped in betel leaves; the combination has mildly narcotic effects, on a level perhaps with drinking coffee. The handle here is in the shape of an areca tendril. Other domestic objects were often placed as offerings on altars or the graves of ancestors; lime-pots, however, though they were respected, even venerated, household objects, were not considered appropriate for temples and graves.

**CAT. 146**

## COVERED JAR

14th–16th century
Glazed highly fired stoneware,
incised cloud and floral designs
5 1/8 x 5 inches
Collection of the Art Fund, Inc. at the
Birmingham Museum of Art; Bequest of
William M. Spencer III AFI170.2010a-b

**CAT. 147**

## BOWL

15th–16th century
Glazed stoneware, the character phuc, "good fortune," painted in underglaze-blue cobalt-oxide
3 1/8 x 5 1/4 inches
Collection of the Art Fund, Inc. at the Birmingham Museum of Art; Bequest of William M. Spencer III
AFI81.2010

CAT. 148

## BEAKER

16th century
Glazed stoneware, four circular bands painted in underglaze-blue cobalt-oxide
4 1/8 x 4 1/8 inches
Collection of the Art Fund, Inc. at the Birmingham Museum of Art; Bequest of William M. Spencer III AFI105.2010

CAT. 149

## BOWL

16th century
Glazed stoneware with circle painted in underglaze-blue cobalt-oxide
2 1/8 x 3 5/8 inches
Collection of the Art Fund, Inc. at the Birmingham Museum of Art; Bequest of William M. Spencer III
AFI106.2010

CAT. 150

## SMALL BOWL

16th century
Glazed stoneware with circle painted in underglaze-blue cobalt-oxide
2 1/4 x 3 1/2 inches
Collection of the Art Fund, Inc. at the Birmingham Museum of Art; Bequest of William M. Spencer III
AFI107.2010

**CAT. 151**

## COVERED BOX

15th–16th century
Glazed stoneware, incised panels
with floral designs
3 ¼ x 4 ⅛ inches
Gift of Dr. William S. Moughan, Jr.
1980.418a-b

CAT. 152

## WATER DROPPER

15th–16th century
Glazed stoneware
with loop handle and spout
3 x 3 1/4 inches
Gift of Mr. Don Marino 1981.191

**CAT. 153**

## LIME-POT

15th–16th century
Glazed stoneware with areca-vine handle
4 7/16 x 4 5/16 inches
Gift of Dr. and Mrs. J. Marshall Garrett
1980.402

CAT. 154–157

# LEAD-GREEN GLAZED WARES

A type of green glaze was developed based on lead rather than iron. It fired to a bright color but was not hard and tended to flake. The molded designs and firing spurmarks that are often found in the wells of bowls with this glaze, for example, the floral motifs in six panels of 155, suggest fourteenth- to fifteenth-century dates of manufacture. Piece 157 may have been used either as a stand or possibly an inkstone. The molded designs are often well formed (the design of bowl 154 seems to have late Yuan or early Ming prototypes) but the glaze type appears not to have been used for long.

CAT. 154

## BOWL

14th–15th century
Glazed stoneware, molded floral scrolls between squared-spiral bands, chrysanthemum in well, lead-green glaze
2 ¾ x 7 ¼ inches
Collection of the Art Fund, Inc. at the Birmingham Museum of Art; Bequest of William M. Spencer III AFI68.2010

**CAT. 155**

## DISH

14th–15th century
Glazed stoneware, molded floral designs
in six panels, lead-green glaze
1 3⁄4 x 6 3⁄4 inches
Collection of the Art Fund, Inc. at the
Birmingham Museum of Art; Bequest of
William M. Spencer III AFI85.2010

## CAT. 156

# BOWL

14th–15th century
Glazed stoneware, molded floral decoration, lead-green glaze
2 ¾ x 7 ¼ inches
Collection of the Art Fund, Inc. at the Birmingham Museum of Art; Bequest of William M. Spencer III AFI92.2010

**CAT. 157**

## STAND

14th–15th century
Glazed stoneware, carved
cut-out base, lead-green glaze
1 5⁄8 x 6 3⁄4 inches
Collection of the Art Fund, Inc. at the
Birmingham Museum of Art; Bequest of
William M. Spencer III AFI178.2010

CAT. 158–164

# CHAM CERAMICS

All the ceramics discussed so far were made in the Red River Valley, in the north of Vietnam, the historic heartland of Vietnam. To the south, along the coast of central Vietnam, was Champa, a loose polity of peoples with a reputation for seafaring and trade. The Viets and the Chams were traditional enemies, and in 1471 the Viets took the Cham capital and extinguished Cham power; they did not extinguish the Cham people, who remain a distinct minority today.

Regarding ceramics, the Cham did not have the advantages of the fine clay of the Red River Valley, or China as neighbors to give them aesthetic and technical inspiration, but they were capable of producing good ceramics. Typical are robust brown-glazed jars, often with strap handles and with applied, carved, or incised designs of dragons or floral patterns (162, 163, 164); larger jars long attributed to Champa may have been made in southern China, or even Laos, for the hill-tribes market.

Some Cham pieces found their way to Indonesia and the Philippines, where bowls with a blue-gray glaze (like 159 and 160) have been excavated in domestic home-sites in association with Vietnamese and Thai pieces dating from the fifteenth and sixteenth centuries. These blue bowls are a common Cham type. A bowl (161) is particularly thin-walled and well potted, with a floral molded pattern in the cavetto; it is more carefully made than contemporary Vietnamese pieces (such as bowls 81–88).

CAT. 158

## BOTTLE

15th–16th century
Glazed stoneware, incised
floral designs
7 ¾ x 4 inches
Gift of Dr. and Mrs. L. Clark
Gravlee 1976.337

CAT. 159

## BOWL

15th–16th century
Glazed stoneware
2 x 5 ½ inches
Collection of the Art Fund, Inc. at the Birmingham Museum of Art; Bequest of William M. Spencer III AFI113.2010

## CAT. 160

# BOWL

15th–16th century
Glazed stoneware, incised lines on
exterior to suggest fluting or carved petals
2 1/4 x 5 5/8 inches
Collection of the Art Fund, Inc. at the
Birmingham Museum of Art; Bequest of
William M. Spencer III AFI114.2010

**CAT. 161**

## BOWL

15th–16th century
Glazed stoneware, molded floral design around lower part of cavetto, molded flower in well
2 ½ x 6 ⅛ inches
Collection of the Art Fund, Inc. at the Birmingham Museum of Art; Bequest of William M. Spencer III AFI110.2010

**CAT. 162**

## JAR

16th–17th century
Glazed stoneware, rolled rim,
four strap handles, floral design
carved through brown glaze
12 5⁄8 x 8 3⁄8 inches
Gift of Dr. and Mrs. Lawrence J.
Lemak 1980.414

**CAT. 163**

## JAR

15th–16th century
Glazed stoneware, six carved loop handles, two incised dragons chasing each other over a fish-scale pattern
9 1/8 x 7 3/16 inches
Gift of Mr. and Mrs. Harris Saunders, Jr. 1980.429

CAT. 164

## JAR

16th–17th century
Glazed stoneware, four tiger handles with the character for "king" carved on their foreheads, two applied dragons chasing pearls of wisdom
11 x 9 ½ inches
Gift of The Ferster Collection 1995.143

CAT. 165

# SEVENTEENTH CENTURY

From the seventeenth century onward, the most interesting developments in Vietnamese ceramics were temple wares, which became increasingly ornate and over-decorated, even baroque. The most important types were large blue-and-white candle stands with molded and intricate applied dragons and large rectangular incense-burners (165). The surface of the incense-burner here has applied designs of dragons, clouds, birds, and flowers in molded biscuit. The molding on this type of incense-burner was usually restrained, limited to a clear or cream-colored glaze. Examples similar to 165 in Hanoi and The British Museum have inscriptions that date them to 1634 and 1635.

**CAT. 165**

## INCENSE BURNER

17th century
Glazed stoneware, applied dragons, clouds, birds, and floral motifs in molded biscuit with cream-colored glaze
12 3/8 x 10 x 5 inches
Collection of the Art Fund Inc. at the Birmingham Museum of Art; Gift of the Multiple Sclerosis Foundation in honor of Mr. William M. Spencer III AFI 6.2008

CAT. 166

# EIGHTEENTH CENTURY

The Vietnamese believed that they were descended from dragons, and dragons continued to be favorite decorative motifs for ceramics. The manufacture and painting of this large jar (166) are not equal in quality to the blue-and-white masterpieces of previous centuries, but they remain vigorous and robust. The export trade declined, though the Dutch East India Company continued to ship large quantities of "coarse porcelain" from Vietnam to Indonesia through the seventeenth century. Faced with growing Chinese competition, the English East India Company withdrew from Hanoi in 1698, and the Dutch did the same in 1704.

CAT. 166

## JAR

18th century
Glazed stoneware, two applied dragons chasing Buddhist jewels of wisdom, above band of cloud motifs
16 3/4 x 11 3/4 inches
Gift of Dr. and Mrs. M. Bruce Sullivan 1992.59

**CAT. 167**

# NINETEENTH CENTURY

The four molded and applied Buddha images on a large white jar (167) indicate that it was made for temple use. It may have been made at the Bat Trang kilns outside Hanoi, or possibly at the Sekwan (Shiwan) kilns in southern China and then imported into Vietnam. The gilding is unusual. A long inscription in underglaze-blue mentions a temple named Terrace of Clouds, Yuntai in Chinese. Apart from formal *bleu de Hue,* which were painted in China following Vietnamese designs, larger Vietnamese ceramics produced in the nineteenth century tended to be unique commissions and not follow shape-types.

| | |
|---|---|
| 一鞭惊醒夢迷人 | *One stroke of the whip rouses the sleeper lost in a dream* |
| 三眼最享塵世事 | *The third eye best apprehends the vanity of human affairs.* |
| 雲臺珍古寺 | *The Yuntai's Zhengu Temple* |
| 溪水德禅林 | *The stream and Dechen woods* |
| 靈威超三界 | *The grandeur of the soul transcends the threefold division of the universe* |
| 恩澤濟萬民 | *Gracious favors benefit the myriads of people* |

Translated by Thomas Stewart

## CAT. 167

# JAR

19th century
Glazed stoneware, applied gilded
Buddhas and Bodhisattvas, with
lengthy dedicatory inscription
17 ½ x 15 ¼ inches
Museum purchase with funds from the
Endowed Funds for Acquisitions 2008.101

**CAT.** 168–219

# ADDITIONAL VIETNAMESE CERAMICS FROM THE BIRMINGHAM MUSEUM OF ART

## LY DYNASTY

CAT. 168

### JAR

12th–14th century
Glazed stoneware
8 3/4 x 8 1/4 inches
Gift of Mr. and Mrs. James T. Stephens
1977.238

## GREEN WARE

CAT. 169

### BOWL

14th century
Glazed stoneware
1 3/4 x 6 1/2 inches
Gift of Judge and Mrs. Marvin Cherner
1978.69

CAT. 170

### BOWL

14th century
Glazed stoneware
2 5/16 x 6 1/2 inches
Gift of Dr. and Mrs. Philip Watkins
1978.103

CAT. 171

## JAR

15th century
Glazed stoneware
3 7/16 x 2 3/8 inches
Gift of Dr. and Mrs. Joseph W. Sewell
1982.264

CAT. 172

## BOWL

14th–15th century
Glazed stoneware
4 1/4 x 7 3/4 inches
Collection of the Art Fund, Inc. at the
Birmingham Museum of Art; Bequest of
William M. Spencer III AFI49.2010

CAT. 173

## BOWL

13th–14th century
Glazed stoneware
3 3/8 x 5 1/2 inches
Collection of the Art Fund, Inc. at the
Birmingham Museum of Art; Bequest of
William M. Spencer III AFI130.2010

CAT. 174

## BOWL

12th–13th century
Glazed stoneware
2 ¾ x 8 inches
Collection of the Art Fund, Inc. at the Birmingham Museum of Art; Bequest of William M. Spencer III AFI148.2010

CAT. 175

## BOWL

12th–13th century
Glazed stoneware
2 ¾ x 6 ¾ inches
Collection of the Art Fund, Inc. at the Birmingham Museum of Art; Bequest of William M. Spencer III AFI151.2010

CAT. 176

## BOWL

13th–14th century
Glazed stoneware
3 ½ x 6 ½ inches
Collection of the Art Fund, Inc. at the Birmingham Museum of Art; Bequest of William M. Spencer III AFI154.2010

**CAT. 177**

## BOWL

13th–14th century
Glazed stoneware
3 x 8 5/8 inches
Collection of the Art Fund, Inc. at the Birmingham Museum of Art; Bequest of William M. Spencer III AFI160.2010

**CAT. 178**

## BOWL

13th–14th century
Glazed stoneware
4 1/2 x 7 1/4 inches
Collection of the Art Fund, Inc. at the Birmingham Museum of Art; Bequest of William M. Spencer III AFI161.2010

**CAT. 179**

## BOWL

14th century
Glazed stoneware
4 1/2 x 4 1/2 inches
Collection of the Art Fund, Inc. at the Birmingham Museum of Art; Bequest of William M. Spencer III AFI166.2010

CAT. 180

## BOWL

14th–15th century
Glazed stoneware
2 3⁄4 x 6 5⁄16 inches
Collection of the Art Fund, Inc. at the Birmingham Museum of Art; Bequest of William M. Spencer III AFI171.2010

CAT. 181

## DISH

14th–15th century
Glazed stoneware
1 3⁄8 x 4 1⁄4 inches
Collection of the Art Fund, Inc. at the Birmingham Museum of Art; Bequest of William M. Spencer III AFI174.2010

CAT. 182

## CUP

15th century
Glazed stoneware
2 1⁄2 x 3 7⁄8 inches
Collection of the Art Fund, Inc. at the Birmingham Museum of Art; Bequest of William M. Spencer III AFI177.2010

CAT. 183

## LIME-POT

15th–16th century
Glazed stoneware
1 3⁄4 x 2 3⁄4 inches
Collection of the Art Fund, Inc. at the Birmingham Museum of Art; Bequest of William M. Spencer III AFI184.2010

CAT. 184

## COVER

13th–14th century
Glazed stoneware
1 ½ x 4 inches
Collection of the Art Fund, Inc. at the Birmingham Museum of Art; Bequest of William M. Spencer III AFI159.2010

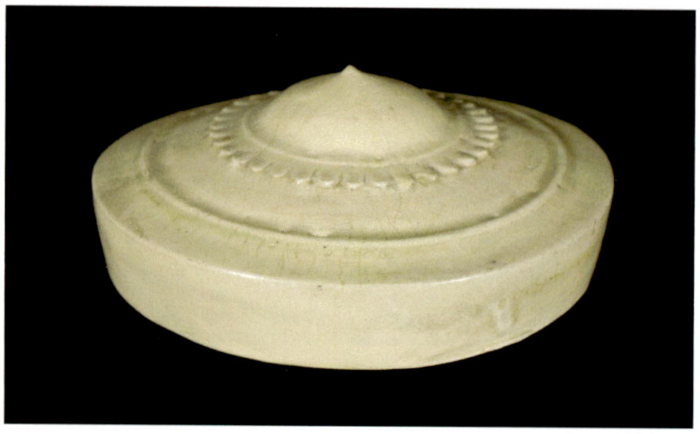

CAT. 185

## COVER

13th–14th century
Glazed stoneware
1 ½ x 2 ¾ inches
Collection of the Art Fund, Inc. at the Birmingham Museum of Art; Bequest of William M. Spencer III AFI190.2010

CAT. 186

## COVER

13th–14th century
Glazed stoneware
1 x 3 ½ inches
Collection of the Art Fund, Inc. at the Birmingham Museum of Art; Bequest of William M. Spencer III AFI191.2010

CAT. 187

## COVER

13th–14th century
Glazed stoneware
1 ½ x 3 inches
Collection of the Art Fund, Inc. at the Birmingham Museum of Art; Bequest of William M. Spencer III AFI192.2010

CAT. 188

## COVER

13th–14th century
Glazed stoneware
½ x 3 ½ inches
Collection of the Art Fund, Inc. at the Birmingham Museum of Art; Bequest of William M. Spencer III AFI193.2010

CAT. 189

## COVER

13th–14th century
Glazed stoneware
1 ⅜ x 3 inches
Collection of the Art Fund, Inc. at the Birmingham Museum of Art; Bequest of William M. Spencer III AFI194.2010

CAT. 190

## COVER

13th–14th century
Glazed stoneware
2 ¼ x 6 ⅝ inches
Collection of the Art Fund, Inc. at the Birmingham Museum of Art; Bequest of William M. Spencer III AFI162.2010

## UNDERGLAZE-BLUE AND WHITE WARE

CAT. 191

### JAR

16th century
Glazed stoneware
with underglaze-blue cobalt-oxide
2 ½ x 2 ⅜ inches
Gift of Mr. and Mrs. George Bargeron and
Mrs. James A. Livingston 1975.80

CAT. 192

### DISH

13th century
Glazed stoneware
with underglaze-blue cobalt-oxide
1 ¼ x 6 ⅜ inches
Gift of Dr. Robert G. Rosser 1976.323

## CAT. 193

# BOWL

14th century
Glazed stoneware
with underglaze-blue cobalt-oxide
2 x 5 ½ inches
Gift of Dr. and Mrs. Sheridan W. Shirley
1976.331

## CAT. 194

# KENDI

14th–15th century
Glazed stoneware
with underglaze-blue cobalt-oxide
3 ⁹⁄₁₆ x 2 ½ inches
Gift of Mr. and Mrs. James T. Stephens
1977.241

## CAT. 195

# BOWL

14th century
Glazed stoneware
with underglaze-blue cobalt-oxide
2 ¾ x 7 ½ inches
Gift of Dr. and Mrs. John D. Elmore
1978.76

### CAT. 196

## CUP

14th century
Glazed stoneware
with underglaze-blue cobalt-oxide
3 1⁄4 x 2 3⁄8 inches
Gift of Mr. and Mrs. Doug Willey 1979.318

### CAT. 197

## BOWL

15th–16th century
Glazed stoneware
with underglaze-blue cobalt-oxide
2 1⁄4 x 4 7⁄8 inches
Gift of Dr. and Mrs. Constantine D. Morros 1981.198

### CAT. 198

## COVERED BOX

15th century
Glazed stoneware
with blue-black painting
2 7⁄8 x 1 7⁄8 inches
Gift of Dr. and Mrs. James W. Sewell
1981.203a-b

**CAT. 199**

## DISH

16th century
Glazed stoneware
with underglaze-blue cobalt-oxide
1 ¼ x 6 ¼ inches
Gift of The Ferster Collection 1995.142

**CAT. 200**

## BOWL

16th century
Glazed stoneware
with underglaze-blue cobalt-oxide
2 ½ x 6 ⅛ inches
Collection of the Art Fund, Inc. at the Birmingham Museum of Art; Bequest of William M. Spencer III AFI78.2010

## CAT. 201

# CUP

16th century
Glazed stoneware
with underglaze-blue cobalt-oxide
2 1/4 x 3 7/8 inches
Collection of the Art Fund, Inc. at the
Birmingham Museum of Art; Bequest of
William M. Spencer III AFI182.2010

## CAT. 202

# JAR

16th century
Glazed stoneware
with underglaze-blue cobalt-oxide
2 1/4 x 2 3/4 inches
Collection of the Art Fund, Inc. at the
Birmingham Museum of Art; Bequest of
William M. Spencer III AFI183.2010

## CAT. 203

# DISH

16th century
Glazed stoneware
with underglaze-blue cobalt-oxide
1 5/8 x 4 3/8 inches
Collection of the Art Fund, Inc. at the
Birmingham Museum of Art; Bequest of
William M. Spencer III AFI185.2010

**CAT. 204**

## COVERED BOX

16th century
Glazed stoneware with underglaze-blue cobalt-oxide and overglaze enamels
3 x 4 ⅞ inches
Collection of the Art Fund, Inc. at the Birmingham Museum of Art; Bequest of William M. Spencer III AFI186.2010a-b

**CAT. 205**

## COVERED BOX

16th century
Glazed stoneware
with underglaze-blue cobalt-oxide
2 x 3 inches
Collection of the Art Fund, Inc. at the Birmingham Museum of Art; Bequest of William M. Spencer III AFI187.2010a-b

**CAT. 206**

## COVERED BOX

16th century
Glazed stoneware
with underglaze-blue cobalt oxide
1 ⅞ x 2 ⁷⁄₁₆ inches
Collection of the Art Fund, Inc. at the Birmingham Museum of Art; Bequest of William M. Spencer III AFI188.2010a-b

CAT. 207

## JAR

16th century
Glazed stoneware
2 1/2 x 3 7/16 inches
Gift of Dr. and Mrs. Chester C. Brummett
1976.309

CAT. 208

## BOWL

14th century
Glazed stoneware
2 5/8 x 6 5/8 inches
Gift of Dr. and Mrs. John D. Elmore
1978.77

CAT. 209

## BOWL

14th–15th century
Glazed stoneware
2 1/2 x 6 3/8 inches
Collection of the Art Fund, Inc. at the Birmingham Museum of Art; Bequest of William M. Spencer III AFI75.2010

CAT. 210

## OFFERING PLATE

11th–13th century
Glazed stoneware
1 x 4 1/8 inches
Collection of the Art Fund, Inc. at the Birmingham Museum of Art; Bequest of William M. Spencer III AFI135.2010

CAT. 211

## BOWL

12th–13th century
Glazed stoneware
4 3/4 x 8 1/2 inches
Collection of the Art Fund, Inc. at the Birmingham Museum of Art; Bequest of William M. Spencer III AFI147.2010

CAT. 212

## VASE

14th century
Glazed stoneware
3 1/2 x 3 15/16 inches
Collection of the Art Fund, Inc. at the Birmingham Museum of Art; Bequest of William M. Spencer III AFI168.2010

## CAT. 213

## BOWL (CHAM)

15th–16th century
Glazed stoneware,
remnants of blue glaze
2 5⁄8 x 3 3⁄4 inches
Collection of the Art Fund, Inc. at the Birmingham Museum of Art; Bequest of William M. Spencer III AFI179.2010

## CAT. 214

## DISH

14th–15th century
Glazed stoneware
1 1⁄4 x 4 3⁄4 inches
Collection of the Art Fund, Inc. at the Birmingham Museum of Art; Bequest of William M. Spencer III AFI189.2010

## CAT. 215

## BOWL

13th–14th century
Glazed stoneware
2 5⁄8 x 6 1⁄4 inches
Collection of the Art Fund, Inc. at the Birmingham Museum of Art; Bequest of William M. Spencer III AFI165.2010

CAT. 216

## BOWL

14th–15th century
Glazed stoneware
2 ¾ x 6 ¾ inches
Gift of Dr. and Mrs. Thomas A. S. Wilson
1980.449

CAT. 217

## BOTTLE

15th century
Glazed stoneware
6 1/4 x 3 9/16 inches
Gift of Dr. and Mrs. Thomas Allen
1980.391

CAT. 218

## BOWL

14th–15th century
Glazed stoneware
2 3/8 x 4 inches
Collection of the Art Fund, Inc. at the Birmingham Museum of Art; Bequest of William M. Spencer III AFI176.2010

CAT. 219

## BOWL

14th century
Glazed stoneware
2 ¾ x 9 ¼ inches
Gift of Mr. and Mrs. Doug Willey
1978.100

# BIBLIOGRAPHY

Adhyatman, Sumarah. *Keramik kuna yang ditemukan di Indonesia: berbagai penggunaan dan tempat asal* (Antique ceramics found in Indonesia: various uses and origins), Jakarta: Ceramic Society of Indonesia, 1981.

Aoyagi, Yoji, Gakuji Hasebe, Shiro Momoki, Asako Morimoto, and Ogawa Hidefumi. "Archaeological research of old kiln sites in Vietnam: Preliminary Report." *Journal of East-West Maritime Relations* Vol. 2 (1992): 19–28.

Aoyagi, Yoji. "Asian Trade Ceramics in the Philippines: Ninth to Sixteenth Centuries." *The Journal of Sophia Asian Studies* No. 10 (1992): 143–76.

Aoyagi, Yoji. "The trend of Vietnamese ceramics in the history of ceramic trade with particular reference to the Islands of Southeast Asia." *Journal of East-West Maritime Relations* Vol. 2 (1992): 1–16.

Asian Art Museum of San Francisco. *Thai ceramics: the James and Elaine Connell Collection.* Kuala Lumpur: Oxford University Press, 1993.

Beck, Ulrich. *Vietnamese Ceramics Miniatures.* Zurich: privately printed, 1989.

Borstlap, Sandra. *Keramiek uit Vietnam.* Leeuwarden (Netherlands): Museum het Princessehof, 1993.

Bound, Mensun. *The Hoi An Wreck, Treasures from the Hoi An Hoard.* San Francisco: Butterfield and Butterfield, 2000.

Brown, Roxanna M. *The Ceramics of South-East Asia: Their Dating and Identification, Oxford in Asia Studies in Ceramics.* Kuala Lumpur: Oxford University Press, 1977.

Brown, Roxanna M. *The Ming Gap and Shipwreck Ceramics in Southeast Asia.* Bangkok: Siam Society, 2009.

Brown, Roxanna M., and Sten Sjostrand. *Turiang: a Fourteenth-century Shipwreck in Southeast Asian Waters.* Pasadena: Pacific Asia Museum, 2000.

Bui Minh Tri and Kerry Nguyen-Long. Vietnamese Blue & White Ceramics. Ha Noi: Social Sciences Publishing House, 2001.

Cao, Xuan Ph. *Cham Sculpture: Album.* Hanoi: Social Sciences Publishing House, 1988.

Chau, Hing-wah. *Collected Essays on the Culture of the Ancient Yue People in South China.* Hong Kong: Urban Council, 1993.

Chen, Dasheng. "Chinese Islamic Influence on Archaeological Finds in South East Asia". In *South East Asia and China: Art, Interaction and Commerce : Colloquies on Art and Archaeology in Asia, no. 17, held June 6th-8th, 1994,* edited by Rosemary Scott and John Guy. London: University of London, Percival David Foundation of Chinese Art, 1995.

Coedès, George, and Hope M. Wright. *The Making of South East Asia.* London: Routledge & Kegan Paul, 1967.

Cort, Louise A. "Buried and Treasured in Japan," in *Thai Ceramics: The James and Elaine Connell Collection.* Kuala Lumpur: Oxford University Press, 1993.

Cort, Louise Allison. "In Search of Ceramics in Vietnam," in *Asian Art & Culture,* vol. 7 no. 1 (1994): 44–61.

d'Argencé, R.-Y. L. *Les céramiques à base chocolatée au Musée Louis Finot.* Paris: Ecole Française d'Extrême-Orient, 1958.

de Frontbrune, Loan. "Les Bleus de Hue," in *Le Viêt Nam des royaumes [exposition, Paris, Le Bon Marché Rive Gauche, 1995].* Paris: Cercle d'Art, 1995.

Diem, Allison. "Vietnamese Celadons," in *Chinese and Southeast Asian Greenwares Found in the Philippines.* Manila: Oriental Ceramic Society, 1991.

Diem, Allison I., and Cynthia Ongpin Valdes. *The Saga of the San Diego (AD 1600).* Manila: National Museum of the Philippines, 1993.

Dofflemyer, Virginia. *Southeast Asian Ceramics from the Collection of Margot and Hans Ries*. Pasadena: Pacific Asia Museum, 1989.

Eberhard, Wolfram. *A Dictionary of Chinese Symbols: Hidden Symbols in Chinese Life and Thought*. London: Routledge 1991.

Fox, Robert. "The Calatagan Excavations: Two 15th Century Burial Sites in Batangas Philippines." *Philippine Studies* Vol. 7 No. 3 (August 1959).

Frape, Christopher J. *Burnished Beauty: The Art of Stone in Early Southeast Asia*. Bangkok: Orchid Press, 2000.

Fukuoka Art Museum. *Vietnamese Ceramics Exhibition*. Fukuoka: Fukuoka Art Museum, 1992.

Fujiwara, Hiroshi, and Dawn Rooney. *Khmer Ceramics from the Kamratan. Collection in the Southeast Asian Ceramics Museum, Kyoto*. Singapore: Oxford University Press, 1990.

Goddard, Dessa. *Treasures from the Hoi An Hoard: Important Vietnamese Ceramics from a Late 15th/ Early 16th Century Cargo,* vols. 1 & 2. San Francisco: Butterfield and Butterfield, 2000.

Goloubew, Victor. "La province de Thanh-hoa et sa céramique," in *Revue des Arts Asiatiques,* 7. Paris: Musée Guimet, 1931.

Gotuaco, Larry. *Chinese and Vietnamese Blue and White Wares Found in the Philippines*. Makati City, Philippines: Bookmark, 1997.

Guy, John. *Oriental Trade Ceramics in South-East Asia, Ninth to Sixteenth Centuries: with a Catalogue of Chinese, Vietnamese and Thai Wares in Australian Collections*. Oxford in Asia studies in ceramics. Singapore: Oxford University Press, 1986.

Guy, John. *Ceramic Excavation Sites in Southeast Asia: A Preliminary Gazetteer*. Adelaide: Research Centre for Southeast Asian Ceramics, 1987.

Guy, John. *Ceramic Traditions of South-East Asia*. Singapore: Oxford University Press, 1989.

Guy, John. "Vietnamese Trade Ceramics," in *Vietnamese Ceramics*. Singapore: Southeast Asian Ceramic Society, 1982.

Guy, John. "Vietnamese Ceramics from the Hoi An Excavation," in *Orientations,* Hong Kong, 2001 (Sept.).

Guy, John, and Rosemary Scott, eds. *South East Asia & China: Art, Interaction & Commerce; Colloquies on Art & Archaeology* in Asia No. 17. London: Percival David Foundation, 1995.

Ha Thuc Can, and Van Huyen Nguyen. *The Bronze Dong Son Drums: A Collective Work of Archaeologists*. Ha Noi: Ha Thuc Can, 1989.

Honda, Hiromu. *Antique Ceramics from the Southern Seas*. Tokyo, 1989.

Honda, Hiromu, and Noriki Shimazu. *Vietnamese and Chinese Ceramics Used in the Japanese Tea Ceremony*. Singapore: Oxford University Press, 1993.

Hubert, J-F. *L'Ame du Viêt Nam:* [Exposition, Paris, Le Bon Marché-Rive Gauche, 1996]. Paris: Cercle d'Art, 1996.

Janse, Olov Robert Thure. *Archaeological Research in Indo-China*. Cambridge: Harvard University Press, 1947.

Jansen, Eva Rudy, and Tony Langham. *The Book of Hindu Imagery: Gods, Manifestations and Their Meaning*. Diever, Holland: Binkey Kok Publications, 1997.

Japan Society of Oriental Ceramic Studies. *Toyo toji* (Oriental ceramics). Tokyo: Japan Society of Oriental Ceramic Studies, 1970.

Lambrecht, Miriam. *Viêtnam: Art et cultures de la prehistoire à nos jours*. Brussels: Musées royaux d'art et d'histoire, 2003.

Lammers, Cheng, Abu Ridho, and Frank Lammers. *Annamese Ceramics in the Museum Pusat Jakarta*. Jakarta: Himpunan Keramik Indonesia, 1974.

Li, Qingxin, and William W. Wang. Maritime Silk Road. Beijing: China Intercontinental Press, 2006.

Locsin, L., & Locsin, C. *Oriental Ceramics Discovered in the Philippines.* Rutland, VT: Tuttle, 1974.

Loviny, C. *The Pearl Road: Tales of Treasure Ships.* Makati City, Philippines: Asiatype and C. Loviny, 1996.

Machida Municipal Museum. *Ceramics of the Indochina Peninsula.* Machida City: The Museum, 1990.

Machida Municipal Museum. *Vietnamese, Thai and Khmer Ceramics.* Machida City: The Museum, 1994.

Machida Municipal Museum. *Khmer Ceramics.* Machida City: The Museum, 1995.

Machida Shiritsu Hakubutsukan. *Tai Mesotto Shutsudo Midorie no Utsuwa: Kokubu Takao Korekushon (The White and Green Wares Excavated in Tak).* Machida Shiritsu Hakubutsukan zuroku, dai 100-shu. Machida-shi: Machida shiritsu hakubutsukan, 1995.

Machida Municipal Museum. *Vietnamese Blue-&-Whites.* Machida City: The Museum, 2001.

May, Jochen, and S. Schulenburg. *Die Nachbarn im Suden: Fruhe Keramik und Bronze aus Vietnam.* Frankfurt am Main: Museum fur Kunsthandwerk, 1999.

May, Jochen. Verborgene Schatze: *2000 Jahre Vietnamesische Keramik* (Hidden Treasures : 2000 Years of Vietnamese Ceramics). Berlin: Museum fur Ostasiatische Kunst, 2000.

Medley, Margaret. *The Chinese Potter: A Practical History of Chinese Ceramics.* New York: Scribner, 1976.

Mikami, Tsugio. *Ceramic Art of the World,* vol. 16. Tokyo: Shogakukan, 1984.

Morimoto Asako, and Kazuo Yamasaki. *Technical Studies on Ancient Ceramics Found in North and Central Vietnam.* Fukuoka: Morimoto Asako, 2001.

Nezu Institute of Fine Arts. *Nanban, Shimamono: Nankai Shorai no Chato.* Tokyo: The Museum, 1993.

Nguyen Dinh Chien. *Cam Nang Do Gom Viet Nam Co Minh Van: The Ky XV–XIX* (Handbook of Vietnamese Ceramics with Inscriptions from the Fifteenth to Nineteenth Centuries). Ha Noi: National Museum of Vietnamese History, 1999.

Nguyen Dinh Chien and Pham Quoc Quan. *Gom Hoa Nau Viet Nam* (Vietnamese Brown Patterned Ceramics). Ha Noi: National Museum of Vietnamese History, 2005.

Nguyen, K. V. *Vietnam: A Long History. Knowledge of Vietnam.* Hanoi: Foreign Languages Publishing House, 1987.

Nguyen-Long, Kerry. "An Indonesian Collection: Vietnam's Painted Ceramics," in *Arts of Asia* 34, Hong Kong, 2004 (March–April).

Nguyen, Quan, & Phan, C. T. *Dieu khac co dien Viet Nam* (Vietnamese Classical Sculpture). Ho Chi Minh City: Tre, 1992.

Nguyen T. T., Minh C., and Vien Triet Hoc. *History of Buddhism in Vietnam.* Ha Noi: Social Sciences Publishing House, 1992.

Nguyen, Trung Son. "Bleu de Hue." *Arts of Asia* 23/3.

Pelley, Patricia M. "Problems in Vietnam History." Southeast Asian Studies Summer Institute, 1992.

Phan Huy Le. *Bat Trang Ceramics 14th–19th Centuries.* Ha Noi: Gioi Publishers, 1995.

Phan, Huy Le, Dinh Chien Nguyen, and Quang Ngoc Nguyen. Gom Bat Trang, the ky XIV-XIX (Bat Trang Ceramics, 14th-19th Centuries). Ha Noi: The gioi, 1995.

Pope, Frank. *Dragon Sea.* Orlando: Harcourt, 2007.

Rawson, Philip S. *The Art of Southeast Asia: Cambodia, Vietnam, Thailand, Laos, Burma, Java, Bali.* New York: F. A. Praeger, 1967.

Reid, Anthony. *Southeast Asia in the Age of Commerce, 1450-1680*. New Haven: Yale University Press, 1988.

Reid, Anthony. *Charting the Shape of Early Modern Southeast Asia*. Singapore: Institute of Southeast Asian Studies, 1999.

Richelieu, Druout. *Vietnam, 3000 ans d'Art,* Paris: ArtComAgency, 2010.

Schafer, Edward H. *The Vermilion Bird: Tang Images of the South*. Berkeley: University of California Press, 1967.

Schafer, Edward H. *The Golden Peaches of Samarkand: a Study of Tang Exotics*. Berkeley: University of California Press, 1985.

Shaw, J. C. *Introducing Thai Ceramics, also Burmese and Khmer*. Chiang Mai: Duangphorn Kemasingki, 1988.

Soothill, William Edward, and Lewis Hodous. *A Dictionary of Chinese Buddhist Terms: with Sanskrit and English Equivalents and a Sanskrit-Pali Index*. London: K. Paul, Trench, Trubner & Co, 1937.

Stevenson, John. "An Introduction to Ly and Tran Monochromes," in *Arts of Asia* 21/3, 1991.

Stevenson, John. "Vietnamese Stoneware Ewers of the Ly and Tran Dynasties," in *Bulletin of the Oriental Ceramic Society of Hong Kong* 9, Hong Kong, 1992.

Stevenson, John, and John Guy. *Vietnamese Ceramics: A Separate Tradition*. Chicago: Art Media Resources, 1997.

Tan, R. C. *Chinese and Southeast Asian greenware found in the Philippines*. Manila: Oriental Ceramic Society of the Philippines, 1991.

Tang, Ba Hoanh, and Dinh The Dang. Gom Chu Dau. Hai Hung, Vietnam: Bao tang Hai Hung, 1993.

Tang, Ba Hoanh, and Dinh The Dang. *Gom Chu Dau* (Chu Dau Ceramics). Ha Noi: Kinh Books, 1999.

Taylor, Keith Weller. *The Birth of Vietnam*. Berkeley: University of California Press, 1983.

Tichane, R. *Ash Glazes*. Iola, Wis: Krause Publications, 1998.

Tingley, Nancy. *Arts of Ancient Vietnam: From River Plain to Open Sea*. New York: Asia Society, and Houston: Museum of Fine Arts, 2010.

Tokyo Kokuritsu Hakubutsukan. *Tokubetsuten kissho: Chugoku bijutsu ni komerareta imi*. Tokyo: Tokyo kokuritsu hakubutsukan, 1998.

Tokyo National Museum. *Jixiang: Auspicious Motifs in Chinese Art*. Tokyo: Tokyo National Museum, 1998.

Tregear, Mary. *Song Ceramics*. New York: Rizzoli, 1982.

Truong, Philippe. *The Elephant and the Lotus: Vietnamese Ceramics in the Museum of Fine Arts, Boston*. Boston, Mass: MFA Publications, 2007.

Turner, Jane, ed. *The Dictionary of Art,* vols. 1–34. London: Macmillan, 1996.

Wibisono, Naniek. *Vietnamese Ceramics from Archaeological Sites in Indonesia*. Tokyo, 1993.

Willets, William Y. *Ceramic Art of Southeast Asia*. Singapore: National Museum, 1971.

Williams, C. A. S. *Outlines of Chinese Symbolism and Art Motives*. Rutland, VT: Tuttle, 1974.

Wright, Arthur F., and Denis Crispin Twitchett. *Perspectives on the Tang*. New Haven: Yale University Press, 1973.

Young, Carol M., Marie-France Dupoizat, and Elizabeth W. Lane. *Vietnamese Ceramics*. Singapore: Southeast Asian Ceramic Society, 1982.

Zetterquist, Eric J. *Vietnamese Ceramics*. New York: Eric J. Zetterquist, 1995.

Zetterquist, Eric J. *Thai and Burmese Ceramics*. New York: Eric J. Zetterquist, 1996.

## AUCTION CATALOGUES

Arts d'Asie: Collection Ho Dinh Art Du Vietnam. Loudmer Commissaires Priseurs S.C.P. Paris: Hotel Drouot, Salle 8 (12 Dec. 1996).

Art d'Asie. Christie's. Paris: 9, Avenue Matignon. (19 Nov. 2003).

Art du Vietnam. Binoche. Paris: Hotel Drouot, Salle 7 (17 Feb. 1995). 265

Art du Vietnam. Collection De S. A. I. Le Prince Bao Long. Binoche. Paris: Hotel Drouot, Salle 6. (22 Nov. 1995).

Art du Vietnam. Collection Nam Phuong, Collection Ha Tuc Can, Ancienne Collection Piccus. Binoche. Paris: Hotel Drouot, Salle 6 (3 Juin 1996).

Important Annamese Ceramics: Robert P. Piccus Collection. Christie's. London (December 1984).

Tek Sing Treasures. Nagel Auctions. (Nov. 2000).

Treasures from the Hoi An Hoard: Important Vietnamese ceramics from a late 15th/early 16th century cargo, Butterfields. San Francisco and Los Angeles (11–13 Oct. 2000).

Vietnam—Studio imaginaire d'un lettre. Paris. Beurdeley & Cie. (19 Jan. 1995).

Ysaguirre, Jose, Charice Silverman, and Susan Paffrath. 2000.